Identifying Special Ne

Identifying Special Needs provides expert guidance to recognising and categorising the specific characteristics of a range of special needs. Drawing on her experience as an educational psychologist and special education teacher, Glynis Hannell provides easy-to-use checklists to help teachers quickly and accurately gather information to determine whether individual students need specialised attention and services, and guidelines on how to provide this help.

This unique book offers diagnostic criteria and supporting notes for a wide range of special educational needs, including autism spectrum disorders, communication disorders, social and emotional issues, cognitive disabilities and specific learning disorders. Relevant to both primary and secondary school students, all checklists can be photocopied for ease of use and downloaded from the companion website. This fully revised third edition includes additional information on guiding conversations with parents, children and colleagues, as well as advice to parents on how to select outside professionals.

The practical checklists and resources help teachers and educational professionals to:

Identify and understand special needs

- screen any student for possible special needs;
- understand the causes and characteristics of various types of special needs;
- link classroom observations to diagnostic criteria used by specialists.

Profile individual differences

- create accurate and comprehensive profiles for individual students, including positive characteristics;
- record each student's unique pattern of development within a special needs 'label'.

Work together with colleagues and parents

- quickly record important information and avoid writing time-consuming reports;
- request and prepare for further assessment and intervention;

- coordinate information from several teachers or professionals;
- involve parents in observing and discussing their child's pattern of strengths and challenges;
- plan effective, inclusive intervention in the classroom setting;
- follow up with recommended further reading, websites and professional references.

Based on internationally accepted diagnostic criteria, and relevant for educational professionals worldwide, this is an essential book for teachers, psychologists and other specialists to ensure that the children and adolescents in their care receive the support they need to succeed.

Glynis Hannell is an educational consultant and award-winning author. She has previously published with Routledge and David Fulton.

Identifying Special Needs

Diagnostic Checklists for Profiling Individual Differences

Third edition

Glynis Hannell

Routledge
Taylor & Francis Group

LONDON AND NEW YORK

Third edition published 2019
by Routledge
2 Park Square, Milton Park, Abingdon, Oxon OX14 4RN

and by Routledge
711 Third Avenue, New York, NY 10017

Routledge is an imprint of the Taylor & Francis Group, an informa business

© 2019 Glynis Hannell

The right of Glynis Hannell to be identified as author of this work has been asserted by her in accordance with sections 77 and 78 of the Copyright, Designs and Patents Act 1988.

First edition published by Corwin Press 2005

Second edition published by Routledge 2014

British Library Cataloguing in Publication Data
A catalogue record for this book is available from the British Library

Library of Congress Cataloging in Publication Data
Names: Hannell, Glynis, author.
Title: Identifying special needs : diagnostic checklists for profiling
    individual differences / Glynis Hannell.
Description: Third edition. | Milton Park, Abingdon, Oxon ; New
    York, NY : Routledge, 2019.
Identifiers: LCCN 2018005052 (print) | LCCN 2018006453
    (ebook) | ISBN 9781351011372 | ISBN 9781138491083
    (hardback) | ISBN 9781138491090 (pbk.)
Subjects: LCSH: Children with disabilities—Education. | Needs
    assessment. | Ability—Testing.
Classification: LCC LC4019 (ebook) | LCC LC4019 .H363 2019
    (print) | DDC 371.9—dc23
LC record available at https://lccn.loc.gov/2018005052

ISBN: 978-1-138-49108-3 (hbk)
ISBN: 978-1-138-49109-0 (pbk)
ISBN: 978-1-351-01137-2 (ebk)

Typeset in Bembo
by Swales & Willis, Exeter, Devon, UK

Visit the companion website: www.routledge.com/cw/hannell

Contents

CHAPTER 1

Introduction

Policy and politics

Motivated by the need to provide appropriate educational opportunities and ensure freedom from discrimination, nations around the world have developed similar approaches to identifying and supporting students with special needs. This reflects the established international standards encapsulated in documents such as the United Nations *Convention on the Rights of the Child* (1989) and the *Salamanca Statement and Framework for Action on Special Needs Education* (1994).

The provision of appropriate education for students with special needs is determined by government policy and enacted by law. Laws relating to special needs generally focus on the obligation to provide every student with an appropriate, inclusive education in the least restrictive environment possible.

Whilst policy framework and funding for special needs depends on legislative changes, such changes are almost invariably driven by an evolving, professional and community understanding of what constitutes best practice in identifying and then meeting the special needs of students.

From time to time governments amend the laws to reflect these changing ideas. In the United States the Individuals with Disabilities Education Act (IDEA) passed in the United States Congress 1990 was superseded by the Individuals with Disabilities Education Improvement Act in 2004. In 2015 Every Student Succeeds Act (ESSA) replaced the No Child Left Behind (NCLB) Act of 2002.

In the United Kingdom the Department for Education and Department of Health jointly issued the Special Educational Needs and Disability Code of Practice (2014). This introduced very significant changes to the provision of special education and associated health and social services in the United Kingdom. The National Curriculum (2013) brought further policy direction to the way in which teaching and learning was approached for all students. The Children and Families Act (2014) contributed further to the changing landscape.

However, it has to be said that there is often a disparity between the ideals set out in the legislation and the level of funding, resourcing and expertise available to support special needs students, their families and their teachers at their local level.

Meeting special educational needs: general principles

Despite variations in policies and inadequacies in resourcing there are also common characteristics in good practice around the world. The contents of this book facilitate the pursuit of good practice.

Parents and their children participate in decision making

The right of parents to play an active part in the development of an appropriate program for their own child is universally reflected in governments' special education policies and practices. Similarly, students themselves have the right to contribute, where possible, to the decisions made regarding their own education.

There is now acknowledgement that the students and their families are not passive recipients of services determined by 'experts' but essential contributors to the process of negotiating an appropriate, effective and acceptable program to address their individual special needs.

The checklists in this book are designed to be 'user friendly' for parents and where practicable their children. Discussion guides are provided to facilitate structured conversations with parents and students. The recommended reading and websites can be useful resources for parents. A guide to help parents avoid untrustworthy, private 'therapists' is provided.

Education is inclusive and individualized

In the past students with special needs were often segregated into special schools or classrooms and in extreme cases not provided with any education at all. Today it is given that every student is entitled to an inclusive education. Unless there are very special circumstances it would be expected that a student with special needs will attend their local school and be placed within the regular classroom.

All students, with and without identified special needs, are unique individuals. It is recognized that teachers are at their most effective when they differentiate their teaching and the classroom program to respond to these individual differences.

The checklists in this book help to collate information about each student's unique pattern of strengths and difficulties and facilitate a formal diagnosis if this is applicable.

The student's eligibility for resources such as additional teaching assistance, equipment or specialist therapy will be assessed on the basis of their identified needs, including information generated by the checklists.

Professionals supporting students with Special Educational Needs

Classroom teachers

Without doubt the key professional for a student with Special Educational Needs is their class teacher. This is the person who will have most contact with the student and who will, generally, have the primary responsibility for ensuring that the student receives an inclusive, individualized program which is appropriate to their needs. Classroom teachers are supported by more specialist colleagues as appropriate.

Specialist teachers and educational advisors

Specialist teachers and educational advisers have very important roles to play in ensuring that students' special needs are fully addressed. Their titles seem to change on a regular basis and they go by different names in different countries. For instance, in the UK they are currently called Special Educational Needs Coordinators (SENCOs) and in the United States they are called Specialist Instructional Support Personnel (SISP). Specialist teachers and advisors may be within the school or may be supporting several schools in the same district.

Medical and other specialists

School psychologists, student counsellors, speech and language therapists, physiotherapists, paediatricians, psychiatrists, social workers and other experts are likely to be part of the advisory team.

Information about the medical and other specialists who may be involved in various categories of Special Educational Need are given in the supporting notes which follow each checklist. In the UK the integration of Education and Health Services is underpinned by the Special Educational Needs and Disability Code of Practice (2014).

Diagnosing and profiling Special Educational Needs

In our efforts to treat every student as an individual there is sometimes a reluctance to use diagnostic categories or 'labels' for fear that we will then 'box' the child or adolescent into a stereotype.

This does both us and the student a disservice. In just the same way that we would expect our medical doctor to treat us as an individual but also to diagnose our condition correctly, so too students have the right to be correctly diagnosed (where a diagnosis is applicable) and for this diagnosis to be used in combination with an understanding of them as individuals.

The profiles created by the checklists in this book explicitly demonstrate that every child, even with a given 'label', is unique and has their own individual characteristics that need to be considered at every stage of planning, delivering and evaluating their educational experiences.

Using parent and teacher observations as a valuable resource

While formal testing and assessment are important in determining a student's needs, vital information also comes from naturalistic observations made, day in and day out, by parents and class teachers.

Such informal observations can be hard to 'capture' and organize. It is all too easy for valuable information to be overlooked in the assessment process. This need not be the case. The checklists in this book offer a practical and efficient way to record real life observations of parents and teachers. Focused on clusters of specific behaviours the observations help to build an accurate and useful profile of a student's special needs.

Diagnosing Special Educational Needs

A key advantage of a diagnostic 'label' is that it creates an instant opportunity to find out more about the condition from the experts in that field. There is a wealth of reliable, evidence-based information available from reputable sources such as scientific journals, researchers, academics and recognized professional experts in their field.

References to scientific articles and books, recommendations for further reading and information on trustworthy websites are provided in the supporting notes which follow each checklist.

Profiling Special Educational Needs

Every student diagnosed with any type of special need has their own unique profile within that category of special need. Identifying a student's unique profile of strengths and special needs is an essential beginning point for the teacher and the specialist advisors.

The checklists provided in this book allow for a broad diagnostic category to be identified and then for the student's unique profile within that category to be mapped out.

The diagnostic checklists

Soundly based and consistent with international diagnostic categories

The checklists in this book develop detailed, diagnostic profiles of individual students, capturing the real-life characteristics of the student's disability, disorder or difficulty. The checklists neatly connect the informal observations from home and school with diagnostic criteria used by specialists.

The checklists are all soundly based on current research and have been refined in consultation with paediatricians, child psychiatrists, psychologists, speech pathologists, classroom and special education teachers, parents and caregivers, and organizations dealing with specific difficulties or disorders. They are intended to supplement (but not replace) standardized tests and assessment tools that may be used in determining a student's special needs.

The checklists are generally consistent (if applicable) with the *Diagnostic and Statistical Manual of Mental Disorders 5th Edition (DSM-V)* 2013, which is recognized internationally as the standard diagnostic reference. Other international classification systems such as the World Health Organization's *Classification of Functioning, Disability and Health for Children and Youth (ICF-CY)* 2007 are also reflected, where appropriate, within the text.

The checklists for giftedness, low self-esteem, maltreatment and immaturity do not have a direct link with DSM-V categories but are included as useful and relevant resources for teachers and other professionals.

The checklists can be used for students between the ages of 4 and 18.

Cognition and learning

Communication

Developmental

Autism Spectrum

Social, emotional and mental health

Sensory

Photocopying the checklists

Photocopying single copies of checklists, for use by teachers and other professionals, as described in this book is permitted. Pages which can be photocopied are marked

Using the checklists for preliminary screening

Every professional will sometimes have concerns regarding a student's learning or behavioural difficulties. Often the teacher, in consultation with the parents, will need to make a decision about whether it is necessary to make a referral to the appropriate advisory service or specialist team.

Sometimes parents are the first to question whether their child might have special needs. The parent may approach the teacher with a request that their concerns are followed up within the school system, with a view to making sure that the student receives appropriate help and resourcing.

As a first step the teacher will usually look at the student's pattern of strengths and difficulties, plan appropriate adjustments and intervention within the classroom and monitor the student's response. If that does not resolve the problem the teacher will usually draw on their own experience and expertise, consult with colleagues and parents and consider the next step.

At this stage the experienced teacher may already be wondering about the possibility of a specific category of special need.

Where there is a tentative view that the student may have a disability or special needs, one or more checklists can be used to organize information and provide preliminary screening. This must always be with the proviso that checklists are not intended to be used as primary diagnostic tools. It is important to remember that many conditions have similar characteristics and that specialist assessment is necessary for formal diagnosis.

Professionals need to be open minded about the origin of the observed behaviours, especially at the early stages of identification and assessment, when more information needs to be gathered.

All children are unique, and we need to respect their developmental and cultural diversity. Professionals, parents, and caregivers filling in these checklists will recognize that each individual child may be quite different from the norm and yet have no disorders or difficulties at all. Observed behaviours may be reflections of a child's unique personality, their developmental trajectory, learned behaviours, earlier experiences, deprivation or cultural differences.

However, the checklists can appropriately be used as a preliminary part of the assessment and diagnosis process. The supporting notes can provide teachers with useful background information.

CASE STUDY

Lily's mother approached the teacher with concerns that Lily might have dyslexia. The teacher knew that despite intensive instruction in literacy Lily's progress had been limited.

Recognizing that the Specific Learning Difficulty (Dyslexia) checklist was a screening instrument and not a diagnostic test, the teacher and parent both completed it. This showed that parent and teacher each observed that Lily had particular problems with memory and phonological skills but that she had strengths in motivation and concentration.

This helped the parent and teacher to consider what type of action they could take to help Lily with her literacy. They also decided to seek further advice. A completed checklist, combined with results from class testing, samples of Lily's work and previous school reports was forwarded to the specialist advisor and provided an excellent starting point for further assessment.

Using the checklists for assessment and diagnosis

Teachers and parents will have access to specialists who are able to assess students with special needs, determine eligibility for resources, advise on intervention and provide specialist support.

These specialists will have formal assessment tools such as standardized tests of intelligence, a battery of achievement tests or a diagnostic schedule for a particular disorder such as Autism Spectrum Disorder.

Using a checklist for quick, comprehensive reporting

The advisor will also need information from teachers who have daily contact with the student. They will need to know what the student is like in day to day classroom activities, what problems are the most evident and how teachers rate the difficulties. They will also want to gather structured information from parents and other adults who have contact with the student.

Advisors will of course talk to teachers and will often ask for a report to be submitted to summarize concerns about the student. However, it is all too easy for important information to be bypassed or for seemingly irrelevant details to be overlooked in a general discussion or written report. Similarly, interviews with parents can often suffer the same fate.

The checklists in this book have been specifically designed to collect, organize and structure information from teachers and others into a clinically or diagnostically relevant format. The checklists put a template of specialist knowledge over normal, everyday observations, creating a bridge between the classroom or home and the diagnostic criteria used by specialists in the assessment of special needs.

The degree of severity attributed to various items can also be of significant importance, helping to sift out what are essentially mild problems from those that warrant a more serious response.

CASE STUDY

Mia, 15 years old, was causing concern at home and at school as her behaviour and motivation seemed to have suddenly deteriorated. The specialist who saw Mia asked the three teachers who knew Mia best to complete the Depression checklist.

continued

> Mia's teachers all rated her 'Lack of interest and enjoyment' and 'Social isolation' as moderate or severe, in other areas there was less consistency between their ratings.
>
> Mia's mother highlighted 'Disturbed eating or sleeping patterns'. Everyone agreed 'social isolation' was an extreme problem. As her mother said, 'Rating her at 3 is an understatement!'. This gave Mia's teachers and parents a solid basis for an urgent referral to an adolescent mental health service.

Using the checklists to profile individual differences

Diagnostic labels such as *Intellectual Impairment* or *Specific Learning Disability* can be useful; they can serve as general signposts to the type of difficulties which the student may be experiencing and perhaps help to establish an entitlement to funding or additional support. However, by itself the diagnostic label provides very little useful information about the particular student and their individual needs.

Responding to students' unique, individual differences is at the centre of good practice around the world. It is impossible for teachers to devise an appropriate program for a student with special needs without first understanding the unique, individual profile of that student.

No two students are ever alike. Even when they share the same diagnostic 'label' there will still be many more differences than similarities between them.

One student with a Specific Learning Disability has major difficulties with concentration and motivation, another student with the same disability is focused and confident but has far greater problems with memory, speech and language than his peer.

One student with Autism Spectrum Disorder has severe difficulties with social and emotional empathy but has reasonable communication skills; another student also diagnosed with the same condition has a very different profile and consequently a very different set of educational needs.

Understanding these individual differences is the key to ensuring that effort is directed to the areas of greatest need, that strengths are valued and built on and that there is a good fit between what the student needs and what the teachers and other professionals provide.

A checklist from this book can be used create a practical overview of the student's particular difficulties and strengths. The items encourage adults to focus on particular behaviours or characteristics and to notice the patterns that become evident. This helps to identify individual priorities for intervention, recognizes personal strengths and provides an important basis for planning intervention which is suited to that particular student's individual needs.

CASE STUDY

Ethan and Riley were already identified as having mild intellectual disabilities with similar IQ scores and levels of academic achievement.

The checklists were used to provide a quick and accurate profile of each boy. The completed checklists showed that Ethan was quite independent with self-care and did well socially but his difficulties with learning were significant.

On the other hand, Riley similarly struggled with learning but also found it hard to integrate socially. His play was immature, and he needed a lot more help with self-care than other children of his age. This helped teachers to plan accordingly to meet each boy's individual needs.

Using the checklists to coordinate professional perspectives

In most situations several professionals coordinate their work with each other to achieve the best outcomes for the student with special needs. The checklists can be used to obtain the same set of information from each of the professionals so that direct comparisons can be made.

Once all the individual checklists have been completed points of similarity and comparisons between different observers or different situations can be clarified.

When several people complete the same checklist, it is not unusual for different people to rate the items differently.

One teacher may have concerns about concentration, another may not. A social worker may be aware of a particular behaviour that never occurs at school. The variations in ratings can, in themselves, provide very useful information for professionals, reflecting the complexity and diversity of the individual student's special needs in different settings or in different circumstances.

Supporting notes

The supporting notes following each checklist give food for thought. Could this be something else, with similar characteristics? Could there be more than one problem surfacing at the same time?

Discussion with colleagues

The checklists can also be used as the basis for professional discussions, where a team of teachers work through a checklist together. Asking each person at the meeting to consider the same item often leads to valuable professional discussion about the student and their needs.

A Discussion Guide is provided on page 184 of this book to help professionals coordinate their perspectives.

CASE STUDY

Frankie was often a restless, inattentive student and Attention-Deficit/ Hyperactivity Disorder was being considered. Frankie's class teacher, his science teacher and his previous year's teacher all completed the checklist.

continued

Everyone was in agreement that Frankie was a bright, energetic and very talkative boy. However, there was wide disagreement about his levels of concentration.

Discussing this disparity, Frankie's teachers realized that it all depended on what he was being asked to do. If he was expected to do regular grade work Frankie was easily sidetracked, unwilling to persevere and generally inattentive, but when intellectually challenged or when following his own interests Frankie could show deep concentration.

The gifted and talented checklist was tried and proved to be a much better fit for Frankie!

Using the checklists with parents

The parents' rights to be consulted and to participate as equals in planning their child's education and care are protected by law in all developed countries. Parents can provide essential insights into their child, their difficulties and their strengths.

Parents see their child in a different environment to the school environment, and they can provide crucial information about how or whether the child's difficulties present themselves outside of school. In addition, parents can provide insights about how cultural differences may be affecting the child's school behaviour. Children's behaviour can appear very different when seen from the perspective of the parents, and a wise teacher will make every effort to understand that perspective.

Mutual understanding and joint decision making between parents and professionals will ensure strategies being planned have the best chance of success. Home and school can work together with shared goals. A parent who feels excluded from decision making or who feels alienated by the process of identifying their child's special needs will not be able to support the teachers and other professionals working in the best interests of the child.

The checklists can be used to provide practical frameworks for the essential conversations between teacher and parent.

Discussion with parents

The task of beginning a conversation with a parent about the possibility that their child might have a disability or disorder needs considerable tact. Parents may understandably feel out of their depth, confused or defensive about what is being proposed.

The checklists were designed to help parents and professionals talk on equal terms about the difficulties that a student is experiencing. The language used in the checklist items is deliberately straightforward and does not depend on specialist understanding or vocabulary. This can help to demystify the process of assessment by giving real life examples of the sort of behaviour that leads to a diagnosis of a particular disorder.

Because the checklists are just simple lists, not formal tests or standardized tools, they can be used as a practical basis for a structured conversation with a parent. If appropriate a parent can be given a checklist to complete by themselves, equally teacher and parent can sit together and talk their way through a checklist in a collaborative way.

The structure of the checklist leads the conversation systematically through the student's particular profile of difficulties and strengths. However, there is nothing to stop the parent or teacher talking about other, relevant issues that might come to mind as they go through the checklist. Indeed, using the checklist items as a spring-board for wider discussion can often be very useful.

When a teacher and parent are talking about a student the discussion can cover a wide range of topics and go off at various tangents. A Discussion Guide is provided on page 186 of this book to help professionals prepare a structured conversation with parents or caregivers.

There is also a handout called *Trustworthy or not?* on page 182. This helps parents to check whether any 'therapists' offering private treatment for their child are trust-worthy or not. It is good for teachers and parents to work collaboratively to find the very best help available for the child with special needs.

CASE STUDY

Jack's teacher found Jack to be an engaging but rather unusual student. She used the Asperger Syndrome checklist as a basis for a structured conversation with Jack's mother.

Teacher: I've been thinking a lot about Jack. Could we go through a few things together and see if we are both on the same track?

Parent: Yes, but I don't want him taken out of this school

Teacher: That's fine, we are looking at how to help him right here in his classroom. I looked at this checklist and it rang a few bells for me, and I was thinking we could look at it together, just as a start-ing point. It's not a test, something that might give us a few pointers. You can see it's on Asperger Syndrome. Have you heard of that?

Parent: You're not saying he is retarded are you . . . he's not that . . .

Teacher: No, no! Asperger Syndrome is a name for a type of kid who can be pretty smart . . . I wanted to ask you what you thought. Here's the first part *Has few, if any, friends*. Does that apply to Jack?

Parent: No, he's got couple of nice friends, though not many. I'd give him a 1 for that.

Teacher: What about this one *Makes inappropriate comments or does socially inappropriate things?*

Parent: Oh goodness, last week he went right up to my boss and told she was going to die of obesity . . . he'd seen something on the TV . . . he gave her all the scientific facts and figures. I'd have to give him a 3 for that. He is mad on scientific facts and figures . . . He's a vol-unteer for the local nature reserve; they say he's the best scientist they've got!

Conversations such as this allow parents and teachers to talk factually about the student's individual profile of strengths and difficulties and, in fact, gave Jack's mother a chance to talk on an equal footing with the teacher about Jack's strengths and weaknesses. This created a good foundation for home and school to work together to meet Jack's special needs.

continued

It is of course important for the teacher to stress that the checklist is intended to act as a very preliminary exploration of the student's difficulties and is only the beginning point of working out whether the student has special educational needs and if so how these might best be addressed. The conversation often throws up other, useful information that might not otherwise have emerged.

Sometimes it is the parent who raises the possibility of their child having a special need and once again a suitable checklist can provide a sound basis for the structured conversation between teacher and parent and help provide objective talking points.

Using the checklists with students

Student participation in planning their own educational programs is usually mandated by government. Of course, this is sometimes constrained by the age and capacities of the individual student, but nevertheless it is essential that the student's views are taken into consideration, either by direct engagement with the student and/or working with their parents or other adults able to advocate on their behalf.

It may sometimes (but not always) be appropriate to use a checklist as the basis of discussion either as an informal 'road map' to guide the teacher's choice of topics or as the basis for a structured conversation with the student. In this situation it is essential that the adult has good rapport with the student. The adults can talk through, explain or paraphrase the items to enable to student to respond. Items can be omitted at the adult's discretion.

A Discussion Guide is provided on page 188 of this book to help professionals prepare a structured conversation with the student.

CASE STUDY

It had already been established that Jayden had dyslexia, but his teacher wanted to talk to him about how Jayden felt about this.

Jayden: I'm just rubbish at reading, that's all, and it don't matter because I'm going to be a professional footballer.

Teacher: I'm banking on you for tickets for Chelsea. But let's go through this checklist so you can tell me a bit more about yourself. What about this item here *Has difficulties learning to read, spell or write.*

Jayden : Like I said I'm rubbish at all that stuff, that give me a 3.

Teacher: What about *Produces school work that does not reflect his true ability.* That means you are smarter than it looks from your school work.

Jayden Yeah! I'm not stupid, just rubbish at reading, give me a 2.

Teacher: I agree, you are definitely not stupid. I'll come back to you with some suggestions about how we might be able to get around those reading and writing hassles and see what you think.

Teacher: Here's another one *Has difficulties working as fast as the other students.*

Jayden: Unreal! Mr T. had a real go at me in Science and said I was slacking but honest I was working flat out, but it took me hours to copy the stuff from the book.

Teacher: I was thinking we could ask Mr T to send the notes straight to your computer, would that work for you?

The use of a checklist provided Jayden and his teacher with an objective 'agenda' which gave both of them the opportunity to talk honestly about issues of importance.

Using the checklists to monitor progress

Supporting notes are provided for each of the checklists including suggested strategies for intervention and recommendations for further reading, to assist in decision making about the most appropriate approach to the student's special needs.

Once strategies have been selected and implemented it is important to monitor if the expected outcomes are being achieved. The student's progress needs to be regularly evaluated and refined as necessary.

Some evaluations should be empirical; for example, standardized test results or the achievement of specified behavioural or performance criterion may be used to measure improvements, but other measures are, of necessity, more subjective.

Checklists, used at regular intervals, can be effective in putting teachers' and parents' observations into a structured framework that can be directly compared with previous checklists, giving information on the student's development and evolving needs.

Even if an adult has already completed a checklist, once a period of time has elapsed it is quite appropriate for them to revisit the same checklist and complete it afresh. It is however better not to look at the previous checklist before completing the second or subsequent ones to avoid unnecessary bias.

CASE STUDY

Completion of the Anxiety Disorder checklist had shown that Sam had particular difficulties with separation anxiety, dealing with new experiences and social situations.

Three months later Sam's teacher and parents completed the Anxiety Disorder checklist again. This showed that Sam was much more confident in separating from his parents but remained very cautious in unfamiliar settings. He had been really unsettled by a recent news item on an earthquake. This helped everyone to attune to Sam's particular sensitivities and difficulties.

continued

> Comparing 'before and after' checklists can show where progress has been made and where problems have continued or escalated, providing a useful gauge for the effectiveness of strategies which were being used.

Supporting notes

Each checklist is an efficient and practical diagnostic tool. However, it is strongly recommended that the checklists are used in the context of the accompanying supporting notes.

The supporting notes provide information on:

Characteristics of the disability or disorder

This outlines the overall, typical characteristics of each disorder.

Causes of the disability or disorder

This gives a brief outline on what is known about the causes of the condition, although quite often there may not be a clear-cut cause.

Other conditions which share similar characteristics

This is an important section, reminding readers that one condition can quite easily be mistaken for another. For example, does the child have ADHD or is an anxiety disorder making it difficult for them to cope with the demands of the classroom? Does the child have an intellectual impairment or a language disorder?

Other conditions which often accompany the disability or disorder

When undertaking a preliminary assessment of a student's difficulties it is essential to remain open to the possibility that a student may have several, concurrent disorders. Sadly, the statistics show that having one disability doubles the risk of having another one, so that a child with, for example an intellectual impairment may easily have a second, or even third impairment such as anxiety or a hearing loss.

Professionals supporting the student

While the class teacher will generally carry the main responsibility for meeting the needs of the student, a team approach is quite often required. Professionals with specialist expertise can make a vital contribution towards meeting the needs of an individual student. Parents sometimes arrange their own, private help for their child.

The handout *Trustworthy or not?* on page 182 helps parents to avoid inappropriate private providers.

Suggested strategies for teachers and/or parents

While this book is intended as a diagnostic and profiling resource, general guidelines are provided as a starting point for considering the type of strategies that could be useful.

Recommendations for further reading

There is a wealth of information available on all the Special Educational Needs found in this book. Reading further helps parents and teachers enhance their understanding and so be more able to provide the student with appropriate assistance.

Recommendations for useful websites

There are many websites set up by reputable organisations with information, expertise and resources to support a student, their parents and their teachers. This book provides guidance about the type of information available and where the organisation is based.

References

All of the information in this book has been thoroughly researched, with professional journals forming the mainstay of the author's background reading. The primary references are provided at the end of each set of supporting notes.

Choosing the right checklist

Usually the professional educator will be well equipped to make an educated selection of which checklist(s) may be most appropriate as a starting point. One, well chosen, checklist will usually provide sufficient information, but two or more checklists can easily be used in combination to provide an even fuller picture of a student's day to day challenges. Charts to help readers select the most appropriate checklist(s) are provided on pages 191–4.

Supplementary resources

Chapter 8 includes supplementary resources

Trustworthy or not? *182*

Guide: Discussing a student's special needs with colleagues *184*
Guide: Discussing special needs with parents *186*
Guide: Discussing special needs with a student *188*

Selecting the right checklist *190–4*

References

Baglieri, S. and Shapiru, A. (2012) *Disability Studies in the Inclusive Classroom: Critical Practices for Creating Least Restrictive Attitudes*, New York and Abingdon, UK: Routledge.

Barnes, P. (2008) 'Multi-agency working: what are the perspectives of SENCos and parents regarding its development and implementation?' *British Journal of Special Education*, 35, pp. 230–240.

Blandford, S. (2013) 'The impact of "achievement for all" on school leadership', *Educational Management Administration Leadership*, 41(1), pp. 45–62.

Cook, B. and Cook, S.(2013) 'Unravelling evidence-based practices in special education', *Journal of Special Education*, 47(2), pp. 71–82.

DfE (2013) *The National Curriculum in England. Key Stages 1 and 2 Framework Document*, London: Crown Copyright.

DfE (2014) *The National Curriculum in England. Key Stages 3 and 4 Framework Document*, London: Crown Copyright.

DfE/DOH (2014) *Special Educational Needs and Disability Code of Practice*, London: Crown Copyright.

DfES (2001) *Special Needs Code of Practice*, London: DfES.

Farrell, M. (2012) *Educating Special Children*. Abingdon, UK: Routledge.

Lebeer, J., (2012) 'Re-assessing the current assessment practice of children with special education needs in Europe', *School Psychology International*, 31(3), pp. 69–92.

Miles, S. and Anscow, M. (2010) *Responding to Diversity in Schools: An Inquiry Based Approach*, Abingdon, UK: Routledge.

Mitchell, D., (2014) *What Really Works in Special and Inclusive Education?* Abingdon, UK: Routledge.

Tissot, C. (2013) 'The role of SENCos as leaders', *British Journal of Special Education*, 40, pp. 33–40.

UN (1989) *Convention on the Rights of the Child*, New York: UN.

UNESCO (1994) *The Salamanca Statement and Framework for Action on Special Needs Education*, Paris: UNESCO.

USA Congress (2004) *Individuals with Disabilities Education Improvement Act of 2004*, Washington, DC.

USA Congress (2015) *Every Student Succeeds Act (ESSA)*, Washington, DC.

Cognition and learning

All cognition (thinking) and learning does, of course, depend on how the brain is structured, how it develops and how it functions. The process of brain development is highly complex and depends on many factors. What capacities and predispositions are established well before birth? What subtle differences in the brain's structure or chemistry are associated with specific talents or difficulties? Which factors enhance or damage brain development across the life span?

Scientists have begun to unravel some of these complex questions, so that much is now known and understood about how the brain and its development affects the child and adolescent's ability to think and to learn. However, there are still many unanswered questions about the neurological bases of thinking, understanding, problem solving and remembering.

Cognition and learning occur spontaneously from the early months of life. There is a continuous and dynamic interaction between the brain and the child's environment. New experiences create new neural pathways; potential pathways that are unused atrophy. However, not all brains start the same, neither do all brains develop in the same way.

In this chapter on Cognition and Learning we look at four Special Educational Needs that relate to commonly occurring differences in brain function. These are

INTELLECTUAL DISABILITY CHECKLIST

Glynis Hannell BA (Hons) MSc Psychologist

Name of child or adolescent   Age

Each item should be checked off using the following rating scale

0   Not at all, never occurs, does not apply
1   Mild, sometimes observed, applies to some extent
2   Moderate, often observed, certainly applies
3   Severe, frequently observed, strongly applies

Early developmental delay

Slow to learn to talk	0	1	2	3
Slow to reach physical milestones (walking, sitting, toileting)	0	1	2	3

Needs more help with self-care and everyday living

Needs more help than usual with personal hygiene	0	1	2	3
Needs more adult guidance with personal organization	0	1	2	3
Needs more adult supervision with basic chores	0	1	2	3
Needs more adult supervision to ensure safety	0	1	2	3
Needs more adult supervision with managing money	0	1	2	3

Social difficulties

Finds it difficult to make friends in own age group	0	1	2	3
Gets teased or bullied	0	1	2	3
Is socially naïve, innocent, too trusting	0	1	2	3
Is easily led or set up by others	0	1	2	3
Is uninhibited, speaks or behaves inappropriately	0	1	2	3
Thinks someone is a friend when they are only an acquaintance	0	1	2	3
Believes in Santa, tooth fairy and so on much later than peers	0	1	2	3

Immature play and recreation

Plays with younger age group	0	1	2	3
Likes toys and activities suitable for younger age group	0	1	2	3
Gets frustrated and confused by age-appropriate toys or games	0	1	2	3
Slow to learn and follow the rules in organized games	0	1	2	3

Classroom difficulties

Restless and inattentive in group activities 0   1   2   3
Depends on others for help 0   1   2   3
Needs a lot of teacher attention 0   1   2   3
Gets distressed/uncooperative when tasks assigned 0   1   2   3
Does not ask for help (not aware they are on wrong track) 0   1   2   3

Cognitive and learning difficulties

IQ below 75..0   1   2   3
Makes very slow academic progress in comparison to peers.....................0   1   2   3
Needs learning broken into small stages 0   1   2   3
Needs extra repetition to master new learning 0   1   2   3
Needs concrete, hands-on learning experiences...0   1   2   3
Needs more explicit teaching than most 0   1   2   3
Reading comprehension is poor for age..0   1   2   3
Struggles with age appropriate math 0   1   2   3
Finds abstract concepts difficult 0   1   2   3
Drawing and bookwork is immature 0   1   2   3
Seems to be falling further and further behind as time goes by 0   1   2   3

Additional difficulties or disorders

Speech and language less well developed than peers 0   1   2   3
Physically clumsy...0   1   2   3
Behavioural or mental health issues 0   1   2   3
Physical health problems..0   1   2   3

Positive characteristics and strengths (describe at least 3)

Important notes

This checklist can be used to help diagnose and assess Intellectual Disability. However, several conditions have similar characteristics and there may be a range of explanations for the observations made. Specialist assessment is necessary for a formal diagnosis.

- Supporting notes on Intellectual Disability (pages 20–5)
- Guides for discussions with colleagues, parents and students (pages 184–8)

SUPPORTING NOTES ON INTELLECTUAL DISABILITY
Characteristics of Intellectual Disability

Intellectual Disability is characterized by deficits in thinking, problem solving, abstract reasoning, planning, academic learning and learning through experience. The disability also encompasses deficits in daily living, social and self-care skills. Children and adolescents with intellectual disabilities need more support with learning and daily living than usual for their age group.

Internationally there are various terms for Intellectual Disability. 'Mental retardation' is still in widespread use; 'learning disability', 'cognitive impairment', 'cognitive disability', 'intellectual impairment' and 'intellectual developmental disorder' are also used.

Causes of Intellectual Disability

Intellectual Disability is generally caused by a neuro-developmental disorder which disrupts normal brain development and functioning. Chromosomal abnormalities such as Down Syndrome and Fragile X Syndrome and many other syndromes are present from conception.

Problems during pregnancy include exposure of the baby to toxins such as alcohol (resulting in Fetal Alcohol Syndrome) or drugs. Infections, maternal toxemia, placental insufficiency and other health problems will all impact on the developing child.

Premature birth, low birth weight, an infection (such as herpes simplex type 2) acquired during delivery and birth traumas are also associated with an increased risk of Intellectual Disability.

After birth Intellectual Disability can occur because of head injuries, infections such as meningitis, brain tumours and exposure to toxic substances (such as lead), very extreme deprivation and a range of other causes.

Although so many causes can be listed it is still the case that in many situations no cause for a child's Intellectual Disability can be identified.

Conditions which may be mistaken for Intellectual Disability

Language Disorder

Young children, particularly with a moderate or severe Language Disorder can present as having Intellectual Disability. However, there is a clear distinction between those children who have global developmental delay due to Intellectual Disability and those child or adolescents who have language delay or Language Disorder, when other areas of their development are within the normal range for their age group.

Autism Spectrum Disorder

Intellectual Disability often accompanies Autism Spectrum Disorder. A significant percentage of children and adolescents with autism will also have Intellectual Disability. Clinically, it is a complex issue to identify the exact contribution each of these two significant developmental disorders makes to the child or adolescent's functioning.

Conditions which may occur alongside Intellectual Disability

Intellectual Disability with neurological disorders

Cerebral palsy, epilepsy and other neurological disorders often accompany Intellectual Disability.

Intellectual Disability with Autism Spectrum Disorder

Most children or adolescents with severe Autism Spectrum Disorder will also have Intellectual Disability, although the reverse is not true in that most children or adolescents with Intellectual Disability do not have Autism Spectrum Disorder.

Intellectual Disability with Attention-Deficit/Hyperactivity Disorder (ADHD)

Many children or adolescents with Intellectual Disability also have problems with self-regulating their concentration and impulsive behaviour and have Attention-Deficit/Hyperactivity Disorder (ADHD) along with their Intellectual Disability. Making a distinction between the two conditions can be a difficult and complex diagnostic issue.

Intellectual Disability can mimic the symptoms of ADHD if the child or adolescent is placed in a situation in which the level of difficulty of tasks is too high or the pace of delivery of instruction is too fast. In this case inattentiveness and restlessness may just be a natural response to a situation that is inappropriate to their needs.

Intellectual Disability with behaviour disorders

Children or adolescents with Intellectual Disability can also have a behavioural disturbance such as Conduct Disorder in parallel with intellectual impairments. However, Intellectual Disability can exacerbate or mimic behavioural disorders. Difficulties in understanding instructions, judging a situation and inhibiting responses may lead to inappropriate, possibly unacceptable behaviour.

Intellectual Disability with emotional disorders

Children or adolescents with Intellectual Disability may often experience marked problems coping with the demands of everyday life such as integrating socially and coping with learning, which in turn will create additional stress on the individual. Anxiety is often associated with Intellectual Disability.

Depression and other mental health problems can also exist in parallel with Intellectual Disability without there being a direct causal link.

Intellectual Disability with maltreatment

Children or adolescents with Intellectual Disability are very vulnerable because they tend to be naive and immature and have poor intellectual and social problem-solving skills. They are therefore at much greater risk of being sexually, physically or emotionally maltreated than their peers.

Intellectual Disability with immaturity

One of the diagnostic criteria for Intellectual Disability is that the child or adolescent not only has significant cognitive deficits but also lacks age appropriate levels of personal independence and social participation.

Children and adolescents with Intellectual Disability very commonly show signs of marked immaturity. Overall development may well be delayed so that intellectual development, play preferences, social skills, self-discipline and judgment are all at a level that might usually be expected of a significantly younger child.

Professionals supporting the student (Intellectual Disability)

Teachers

Class teachers and special educators will have a primary role in supporting the child or adolescent with Intellectual Disability.

Psychologists

Psychologists will be involved in the formal assessment of the child or adolescent's intellectual capacities and adaptive functioning. Psychologists may also be involved in providing support in the case of emotional or behavioural disorders that may occur concurrently or develop as a consequence of Intellectual Disability,

Speech pathologists

Speech pathologists may be involved to provide therapy for specific speech and language related difficulties.

Occupational therapists and physical therapists

Occupational therapists or physical therapists may be involved in the provision of specialist therapy.

Paediatricians and other medical specialists

Paediatricians and other medical specialists will have an ongoing role in managing medical issues and may be involved in the treatment of associated problems such as ADHD or epilepsy.

Child psychiatrists

Child psychiatrists may be involved to deal with emotional and behavioural issues that can arise.

Disability specialists

Disability specialists may be involved, particularly when the Intellectual Disability is severe or is accompanied by other disabilities. These professionals may support families in dealing with matters such as sexuality, life skills, social skills, and so forth.

Social workers

Social workers may be involved to support the family. Respite care and additional financial and practical support may be available if needed.

Community and government agencies

There are likely to be community and government agencies offering a range of support services.

Strategies for meeting the student's needs (Intellectual Disability)

- Arrange for regular assessments to track progress, identify areas of particular difficulty and to isolate any areas in which the child or adolescent may have aptitudes or strengths.

- Parents' rights to be involved and consulted are extremely important. Ensure that there are good communications between home and school.

- Set up an individualized education program to meet the child or adolescent's needs.

- Ensure that all factors such as problems with general health, hearing, eyesight and social disadvantage are identified and managed appropriately.

- Arrange for specialist support in areas of specific difficulty, such as speech pathology for poor language skills, therapy for coordination difficulties, and so forth.

- Provide individual or very small group support in core areas of the curriculum such as literacy and numeracy.

- Ensure that instruction is explicit and appropriate to the child or adolescent's developmental levels.

- Identify individual educational needs and set specific, achievable learning goals.

- Offer significantly more opportunities for consolidation and practice than normal.

- Consider the most appropriate, least restrictive class placement.

- Offer additional social support for those who have socialization difficulties. Provide explicit social skills teaching and supported, supervised play opportunities with peers.

- Provide explicit, protective behaviour training to minimize the risk that they will be abused by others

- Pay particular attention to transition points. Start planning early and ensure good negotiation between all involved parties so that the transition between one learning environment and the next is as smooth as possible.

- Ensure that visiting, temporary or specialist teachers are aware of the child or adolescent's special needs.

- Ensure that there are equal opportunities to participate in a range of activities such as school sports and after school activities, clubs and community youth organizations.

- Ensure that the family has appropriate support through school, community, and government agencies

Recommended further reading for Intellectual Disability

Academic Instruction for Students with Moderate and Severe Intellectual Disabilities in Inclusive Classrooms

Author: June Downing
Date of publication: 2010
Publisher: Corwin

Educating Children and Young People with Fetal Alcohol Spectrum Disorders

Authors: Carolyn Blackburn, Barry Carpenter and Jo Egerton
Date of publication: 2012
Publisher: Routledge

Handbook of Research-Based Practices for Educating Students with Intellectual Disability

Editors: Michael Wehmeyer and Karrie Shogren
Date of Publication: 2016
Publisher: Routledge

Life Skills Activities for Special Children

Author: Darlene Mannix
Date of publication: 2009
Publisher: Jossey-Bass

Positive Discipline for Children with Special Needs: Raising and Teaching All Children to Become Resilient, Responsible, and Respectful

Authors: Jane Nelson, Steven Foster and Arlene Raphael
Date of publication: 2011
Publisher: Three Rivers Press

Teaching Literacy to Students with Significant Disabilities: Strategies for the K-12 Inclusive Classroom

Author: June Downing
Date of publication: 2005
Publisher: Corwin

Teaching Students with Moderate and Severe Disabilities

Author: Diane Browder and Fred Spooner
Date of publication: 2011
Publisher: Guilford Press

Useful websites for Intellectual Disability

www.mencap.org.uk
Mencap. Not for profit organization
Information for parents and teachers. UK

www.downs-syndrome.org.uk
The Downs Syndrome Association. Not for profit organization
Information for parents and teachers. UK

raisingchildren.net.au
Raising Children Network. Government information service
Information for parents. Australia

www.thearc.org
The Arc. Not for profit organization
Information for parents and teachers. USA

References for Intellectual Disability

American Psychiatric Association (2013) *Diagnostic and Statistical Manual of Mental Disorders, 5th edition*, Washington, DC.

Brenda, R.J. et al. (2013) 'Math practice and its influence on math skills and executive functions in adolescents with mild to borderline Intellectual Disability', *Research in Developmental Disabilities*, 34(5), pp. 1815–1824.

Brunson McClain, M., Hasty Mills, A.M. and Murphy, L.E. (2017) 'Inattention and hyperactivity/impulsivity among children with attention-deficit/hyperactivity-disorder, autism spectrum disorder, and intellectual disability', *Research in Developmental Disabilities*, 70, pp. 175–184.

Burack, J. (2012) *The Oxford Handbook of Intellectual Disability and Development*, Oxford Library of Psychology, New York: OUP.

de Graaf, G., van Hove, G. and Haveman, M. (2013) 'More academics in regular schools? The effect of regular versus special school placement on academic skills in Dutch primary school students with Down Syndrome', *Journal of Intellectual Disability Research*, 57, pp. 21–38.

Emerson, E. (2003) 'Prevalence of psychiatric disorders in children and adolescents with and without intellectual disability', *Journal of Intellectual Disability Research*, 47, pp. 51–58.

Ergaz, Z. and Ornoy, A. (2011) 'Perinatal and early postnatal factors underlying developmental delay and disabilities', *Developmental Disabilities*, 17, pp. 59–70.

Georgiadi, M. et al. (2012) 'Young children's attitudes toward peers with intellectual disabilities: effect of the type of school', *Journal of Applied Research in Intellectual Disabilities*, 25, pp. 531–541.

Goodman, R. and Scott, S. (2012) *Intellectual Disability in Child and Adolescent Psychiatry, 3rd Edition*, Chichester, UK: John Wiley & Sons Ltd.

Guralnick, M. (2002) 'Involvement with peers: comparisons between young children with and without Down's Syndrome', *Journal of Intellectual Disability Research*, 46, pp. 379–393.

Leffert, J., Siperstein, G. and Widaman, K. (2010) 'Social perception in children with intellectual disabilities: the interpretation of benign and hostile intentions', *Journal of Intellectual Disability Research*, 54, pp. 168–180.

Mackay, D. et al. (2013) 'Obstetric factors and different causes of special educational need: retrospective cohort study of 407 503 school children', *BJOG: International Journal of Obstetrics and Gynaecology*, 120(3), pp. 297–308.

Nader-Grosbois, N. and Vieillevoye, S. (2012) 'Variability of self-regulatory strategies in children with intellectual disability and typically developing children in pretend play situations', *Journal of Intellectual Disability Research*, 56, pp. 140–156.

Neece, C. et al. (2011) 'Attention-deficit/hyperactivity disorder among children with and without intellectual disability: an examination across time', *Journal of Intellectual Disability Research*, 55, pp. 623–635.

Povee, K. et al. (2012), 'Family functioning in families with a child with Down Syndrome: a mixed methods approach', *Journal of Intellectual Disability Research*, 56, pp. 961–973.

Schalock, R. et al. (2009) *Intellectual Disability: Definition, Classification, and Systems of Supports, 11th Edition*, Washington, DC: American Association on Intellectual and Developmental Disabilities.

Shevell, M. (2008) 'Global developmental delay and mental retardation or intellectual disability: conceptualization, evaluation, and etiology', *Pediatric Clinics of North America*, 55(5), pp. 1071–1084.

Skwerer, D.P. (2017) 'Social cognition in individuals with intellectual and developmental disabilities: recent advances and trends in research', *International Review of Research in Developmental Disabilities*, 53, pp. 91–161.

Statham, H. et al. (2011) 'A family perspective of the value of a diagnosis for Intellectual Disability: experiences from a genetic research study'. *British Journal of Learning Disabilities*, 39, pp. 46–56.

Tirosh, E. and Jaffe, M. (2011), 'Global developmental delay and mental retardation: a pediatric perspective', *Developmental Disabilities Research Reviews*, 17, pp. 85–92.

World Health Organization (2007) *ICIDH-2: International Classification of Functioning, Disability and Health – Children and Youth*, Geneva: WHO.

World Health Organization (2013) *International Classification of Diseases, 10th Edition, Clinical Modification*, Geneva: WHO.

GIFTED AND TALENTED CHECKLIST

Glynis Hannell BA (Hons) MSc Psychologist

Name of child or adolescent   Age

Each item should be checked off using the following rating scale

0   Not at all, never occurs, does not apply
1   Mild, sometimes observed, applies to some extent
2   Moderate, often observed, certainly applies
3   Severe, frequently observed, strongly applies

Advanced early development

Very alert as a young infant 0	1	2	3
Walked early..0	1	2	3
Talked early..0	1	2	3
Advanced language as a preschooler...0	1	2	3
Learned to read early 0	1	2	3
Advanced development of mathematical understanding 0	1	2	3
Advanced drawing skill as preschooler...0	1	2	3

High cognitive ability

Scores above IQ 130 on reputable intelligence scales...............................0	1	2	3
Understands abstract concepts ahead of peers 0	1	2	3
Advanced ability to solve complex problems...0	1	2	3
Very quick learner 0	1	2	3

Curiosity

Frequently asks insightful or innovative questions 0	1	2	3
Enjoys factual books, documentaries, museums 0	1	2	3
Questioning, likes deep understanding of a topic 0	1	2	3
Wants to know exactly how things work 0	1	2	3
Initiates own inventions and experiments 0	1	2	3

Advanced academic achievements

Scores at or above the 98th percentile on attainment tests........................0	1	2	3
Excels in reading comprehension 0	1	2	3
Excels in math..0	1	2	3
Excels in written language 0	1	2	3
Excels in science and/or technology 0	1	2	3

Special talents

Outstanding artistic ability...0	1	2	3
Outstanding musical ability..0	1	2	3
Outstanding sporting ability 0	1	2	3

Outstanding imagination or creativity	0	1	2	3
Outstanding building/construction skills	0	1	2	3
Outstanding leadership skills	0	1	2	3
A lateral or innovative thinker	0	1	2	3
Unusual or subtle sense of humor	0	1	2	3

Learning style

When interested, likes to spend a long time on one activity	0	1	2	3
Dislikes short, superficial tasks	0	1	2	3
Has intense interest in a particular topic	0	1	2	3
Dislikes repetition and practice	0	1	2	3
Enjoys novelty and challenge	0	1	2	3
Tends to complicate simple tasks	0	1	2	3
Sees short cuts and wants to use them	0	1	2	3
Conforms to the norm; only excels when this is expected	0	1	2	3
Inconsistent, can excel with right teacher or topic	0	1	2	3

Out of step with own age group

Prefers older friends or adult company	0	1	2	3
Prefers own company	0	1	2	3
Dislikes group work; prefers to work alone	0	1	2	3
Not understood by other children, described as 'weird' by peers	0	1	2	3
Understands complex issues and speaks like a 'professor'	0	1	2	3
Strong sense of justice, takes on difficult causes	0	1	2	3

Emotional and behavioural difficulties

Does not 'tolerate fools gladly'	0	1	2	3
Argues with adults, always has an answer	0	1	2	3
Uses sarcasm when speaking to peers or adults	0	1	2	3
Is easily bored and then becomes disruptive	0	1	2	3

Positive characteristics and strengths (describe at least 3)

Important notes

This checklist can be used to help diagnose and assess gifted and talented. However, several conditions have similar characteristics and there may a range of explanations for the observations made. Specialist assessment is necessary for a formal diagnosis.

- Supporting notes on gifted and talented (pages 28–33)
- Guides for discussions with colleagues, parents and students (pages 184–8)

SUPPORTING NOTES ON GIFTED AND TALENTED

Characteristics of gifted and talented

Some children and adolescents with exceptional gifts or talents show these abilities very readily. They may be high-achievers with obvious, exceptional talents in areas such as language, literacy, music, mathematics, physical performance, spatial reasoning, art, or interpersonal skills.

However, gifts and talents are not always easily identified. Emotional factors such as anxiety or Depression can incapacitate performance and lead to attainments far below intellectual potential. The need to be accepted by peers and conform to the norm can lead to deliberate underachievement and careful disguise of high academic capabilities.

Specific Learning Difficulties such as Dyslexia can have a significant impact on achievements in areas such as reading, spelling or mathematics. In this situation exceptional intellectual abilities may be masked by poor classroom attainments.

Causes of gifted and talented

High intelligence and special talents do have a genetic component. We know that intelligence, musical ability, mathematical ability and many other human characteristics do get passed on from one generation to the next. Having a gifted or talented parent or grandparent increases the child's chances of having similar traits. However, in no way is there a guarantee that the special gifts or talents of one generation will be inherited by the next. Conversely, many children are born with an array of gifts and talents that are quite unexpected in terms of the aptitudes or capabilities of their parents.

The environment at home, in school and in the community can certainly nurture and develop gifts and talents. The interaction of inborn potential and environmental forces can maximize the way exceptional potential develops.

Conditions which may be mistaken for gifted and talented

Autism Spectrum disorders

Asperger Syndrome or Autism may include exceptional gifts in very isolated areas. For instance, Asperger Syndrome may be characterized by an encyclopaedic knowledge about a topic of special interest, such as train timetables, types of dinosaurs, or makes of cars. Autism can occasionally be associated with an extraordinary capacity in mathematical computation, art, music, or another highly specific area.

Conditions which may occur alongside gifted and talented

Although many gifted and talented children and adolescents are happy, successful and productive, they are not immune to a wide range of difficulties and disorders.

Gifted and talented with a Specific Learning Disorder

A Specific Learning Disorder such as Dyslexia or Dyscalculia will cause delay in academic development. The discrepancy between intellectual potential and academic progress can cause considerable distress. In turn, this can damage self-confidence and significantly impact on motivation.

Gifted and talented with Asperger Syndrome

Passionate interest in and exceptional knowledge of a specific topic can be associated with giftedness and with Asperger Syndrome. Sometimes there may be an overlap between the two conditions, at other times an unusual or extraordinary grasp of a topic is simply a manifestation of a very advanced and exceptional intellect.

Gifted and talented with ADHD

Gifted children or adolescents are just as likely as their less able peers to have ADHD. However, very high intellectual ability can also lead to a quick, impatient learning style or a tendency to drift off into an interesting inner, mental world, so that careful diagnosis is required.

Gifted and talented with emotional or behavioural disorders

When exceptional abilities are not recognized and channelled appropriately, the result may be frustration, boredom and inappropriate behaviour.

High intelligence and special talents can lead to a degree of social isolation because of limited common ground between the gifted or talented youngster and their peers. However, good social relationships are the norm, with social isolation the exception.

Children and adolescents with high intellectual ability can understand social, political and environmental threats and other adult themes which may pass others of the same age group by. This can place a heavy load on immature emotional and social resources, increasing the risk of anxiety and Depression.

Gifted and talented individuals of any age may have a strong tendency toward perfectionism. In moderation, this perfectionism helps to achieve a very high level of success. In excess, perfectionism can lead to Depression or anxiety about perceived failures, particularly when self-esteem is bound tightly to achievements rather than intrinsic personal worth.

The label of giftedness can sometimes produce an adverse effect. Negative stereotypes may apply, or unrealistic and overly rigid or high expectations may be set up. Adults may forget that maturity, stamina, persistence, motivation and attitude may be more closely related to chronological age than intellectual capacity. For example, a young child of very high intellectual capacity may still want to play, have fun and share the same social interests as their own age group and not want to engage in serious study in line with their academic- intellectual development.

Professionals supporting the student (gifted and talented)

Teachers

The team of professionals at school, including class teachers, special education coordinators and teaching staff, teaching assistants and school leaders will be involved in providing an appropriate, inclusive program.

Counsellors

School counsellors may provide emotional and social support when needed.

Strategies for meeting the student's needs (gifted and talented)

Strategies for identification

- Consider screening every individual in the class to identify those who are gifted but not yet showing their exceptional capacities.

- Use both verbal and nonverbal tests to identify those who may have exceptional talents in the visual-spatial areas.

- Arrange for a full assessment for any individual showing signs of having exceptional gifts and talents (include those who are described as exceptional at home, but not at school).

Strategies for meeting the student's needs

- Consider that those who are outperforming their peers may still be underperforming relative to their potential and ensure that the curriculum offered is at an appropriate level for their ability.

- Consider vertical age grouping for academic work, matching for intellectual ability and academic achievement.

- Offer support, intervention and accommodation for areas of difficulty such as Specific Learning Disorders.

- Offer a differentiated curriculum including advanced options so that all members of the class can participate, allowing any unidentified gifted and talented students to extend themselves.

- Offer a differentiated curriculum (as above) so that the intellectually gifted can be integrated into the mainstream and remain part of the social group of the class.

- Do not require successful completion of easier work to establish the student's right to an appropriate, advanced curriculum.

- Consider creating extension groups of intellectual peers for learning in a collaborative learning environment.

- Monitor the effect of participation in an extension group. For some, confidence can be better supported by excelling in a mainstream group rather than by participation in a 'gifted' group.

- Encourage participation in extracurricular activities with additional challenges and interests, such as music, dance, art, debating, science clubs or special interest groups.

- Ensure that the label of giftedness does not set up unreasonable expectations. Acknowledge that intellectual gifts and other talents may occur along with age appropriate maturity in other areas such as emotional or social development.

Recommended further reading for gifted and talented

Best Practices in Gifted Education: An Evidence-Based Guide

Authors: Anne Robinson, Bruce Shore and Donna Enersen
Date of publication: 2006
Publisher: Prufrock Press Inc

Comprehensive Curriculum for Gifted Learners, 3rd Edition

Authors: Joyce VanTassel-Baska and Tamra Stambaugh
Date of publication: 2005
Publisher: Pearson

Education of the Gifted and Talented, 6th Edition

Authors: Gary Davis, Sylvia Rimm and Del Siegle
Date of publication: 2010
Publisher: Pearson

Fundamentals of Gifted Education, 2nd Edition

Editors: Carolyn Callahan and Holly Hertberg-Davis
Date of publication: 2018
Publisher: Routledge

Living with Intensity: Understanding the Sensitivity, Excitability, and the Emotional Development of Gifted Children, Adolescents, and Adults

Editors: Susan Daniels and Michael M Piechowski
Date of publication: 2009
Publisher: Great Potential Press Inc

Project-Based Learning for Gifted Students: A Handbook for the 21st-Century Classroom

Author: Todd Stanley
Date of publication: 2012
Publisher: Prufrock Press Inc

Teaching Gifted Children with Special Needs

Author: Dianne Montgomery

Date of publication: 2015

Publisher: Routledge

The Psychology and Education of Gifted Children

Authors: Philip Vernon, Georgina Adamson and Dorothy Vernon

Date of publication: 2014

Publisher: Routledge

101 Success Secrets for Gifted Kids

Useful websites for gifted and talented

www.potentialplusuk.org

Potential Plus UK

Information for parents and teachers. UK

www.nagc.org

NAGC – The National Association for Gifted Children

Information for parents and teachers. USA

www.world-gifted.org

Worldwide Advocacy for Our Gifted Children

Advocacy and support for gifted children. Not for profit organization. USA

References for gifted and talented

Al-Hroub, A. and Whitebread, D. (2008) 'Focus on practice: teacher nomination of "mathematically gifted children with specific learning difficulties" at three state schools in Jordan', *British Journal of Special Education*, 35, pp. 152–164.

Antshel, K.M. (2008) 'Attention-Deficit Hyperactivity Disorder in the context of a high intellectual quotient/ giftedness', *Developmental Disabilities Research Reviews*, 14, pp. 293–299.

Clinkenbeard, P.R. (2012) 'Motivation and gifted students: implications of theory and research', *Psychology in Schools*, 49, pp. 622–630.

Crepeau-Hobson, F. and Bianco, M. (2011) 'Identification of gifted students with learning disabilities in a Response-to-Intervention era', *Psychology in Schools*, 48, pp. 102–109.

Curby, T. et al. (2008) 'The role of social competence in predicting gifted enrollment', *Psychology in Schools*, 45, pp. 729–744.

Hoogeveen, L., van Hell, J.G. and Verhoeven, L. (2012) 'Social-emotional characteristics of gifted accelerated and non-accelerated students in the Netherlands', *British Journal of Educational Psychology*, 82, pp. 585–605.

Litster, K. and Roberts, J. (2011) 'The self-concepts and perceived competencies of gifted and non-gifted students: a meta-analysis', *Journal of Research in Special Educational Needs*, 11, pp. 130–140.

Little, C.A. (2012) 'Curriculum as motivation for gifted students', *Psychology in Schools*, 49, pp. 695–705.

Lu, J. et al. (2015) Comparisons and analyses of gifted students' characteristics and learning methods. *Gifted Education International*, 33(1), pp. 45–61.

Montgomery, D. (Ed.) (2009) *Able, Gifted and Talented Underachievers, 2nd Edition*, Chichester, UK: John Wiley & Sons Ltd.

Morgan, A. (2007) 'Experiences of a gifted and talented enrichment cluster for pupils aged five to seven', *British Journal of Special Education*, 34, pp. 144–153.

O'Connor, J. (2012) 'Is it good to be gifted? The social construction of the gifted child', *Children & Society*, 26, pp. 293–303.

Preckel, F., Götz, T. and Frenzel, A. (2010) 'Ability grouping of gifted students: effects on academic self-concept and boredom', *British Journal of Educational Psychology*, 80, pp. 451–472.

Reis, S. and Renzulli, J. (2010) 'Is there still a need for gifted education? An examination of current research', *Learning and Individual Differences*, 20(4), 308–317.

Zeider, M. and Matthews, G. (2017) 'Emotional intelligence in gifted students', *Gifted International*, 33(2), pp. 163–182.

DYSLEXIA (SPECIFIC LEARNING DISORDER) CHECKLIST

Glynis Hannell BA (Hons) MSc Psychologist

Name of child or adolescent   Age

Each item should be checked off using the following rating scale

0   Not at all, never occurs, does not apply
1   Mild, sometimes observed, applies to some extent
2   Moderate, often observed, certainly applies
3   Severe, frequently observed, strongly applies

Memory difficulties

Difficulties remembering instructions 0	1	2	3
Problems learning sequences such as multiplication tables 0	1	2	3
Confuses sequences (days of the week, alphabet, numbers) 0	1	2	3
Often makes mistakes when copying words or numbers 0	1	2	3

Speech, phonological and language difficulties

Poor at recognizing individual sounds within a word 0	1	2	3
Poor at recognizing or producing rhymes...0	1	2	3
Poor at recognizing or producing alliteration 0	1	2	3
Difficulties with 'word finding' when speaking...0	1	2	3
Mispronounces words, for example 'hostipal' 0	1	2	3
Later than average in learning to talk 0	1	2	3

Reading difficulties

Difficulties in using phonics to read words..0	1	2	3
Difficulties in learning basic sight words 0	1	2	3
Problems remembering words from one page to the next 0	1	2	3
Slow and hesitant reading despite plenty of practice 0	1	2	3
Loses place when reading; uses finger to keep track...................................0	1	2	3
Reads words that are not there..0	1	2	3
Poor reading comprehension even when reading fluently.............................0	1	2	3

Spelling difficulties

Repeats same spelling mistakes over and over again..................................0	1	2	3
Learns spelling for a test but forgets the words very rapidly 0	1	2	3
Incorrect sounds in spelling, for example 'spun' for 'spoon'.........................0	1	2	3
Spells the same word several different ways...0	1	2	3
Does not recognize spelling that 'looks wrong' 0	1	2	3

Difficulties combining spoken and written language

Difficulties in learning the link between sounds and written letters 0   1   2   3
Can spell a word verbally but cannot write it down 0   1   2   3
Difficulties in getting thoughts on paper..0   1   2   3
Written language is poorly structured..0   1   2   3

Difficulties with handwriting and bookwork

Difficulties with handwriting 0   1   2   3
Bookwork is untidy...0   1   2   3
Mixes upper and lowercase letters..0   1   2   3
Works more slowly than others of the same age 0   1   2   3
Reverses letters and numbers after the age of 7...0   1   2   3
Difficulties with sustained writing; hand gets tired very quickly 0   1   2   3

Underachievement

Literacy skills poor given their age and ability...0   1   2   3
Slow progress in literacy despite appropriate teaching................................0   1   2   3
Achievements and progress do not reflect the effort put in..........................0   1   2   3

Difficulties with motivation and confidence

Low confidence in literacy...0   1   2   3
Avoids learning tasks 0   1   2   3
Low motivation in literacy activities 0   1   2   3
Gets frustrated and upset with literacy activities 0   1   2   3

Positive characteristics and strengths (describe at least 3)

Important notes

This checklist can be used to help diagnose and assess Dyslexia. However, several conditions have similar characteristics and there may a range of explanations for the observations made. Specialist assessment is necessary for a formal diagnosis.

- Supporting notes on Dyslexia (pages 36–41)
- Guides for discussions with colleagues, parents and students (pages 184–8)

SUPPORTING NOTES ON DYSLEXIA

Characteristics of Dyslexia

Dyslexia is a Specific Learning Disorder. It is marked by significant difficulties in the acquisition of basic skills in reading or written language. These difficulties occur despite adequate instruction and normal intelligence. It is often said that Dyslexia causes 'unexpected' difficulties in acquiring and using literacy skills. The child, adolescent or adult with Dyslexia may seem to have every characteristic and circumstance of a potentially successful learner but despite this has significant difficulties with reading and written language.

Dyslexia is a neurodevelopmental disorder where there is a dysfunction in one or more of the neurological processes that underpin the acquisition of literacy skills.

Poor memory is often a major component of Dyslexia and results in significant difficulties in remembering basics which have been taught over and over. Errors may persist despite extensive amounts of appropriate instruction and practice. For instance, the same spelling words may be practiced week after week with little evidence of permanent learning. The sounds of letters may be taught intensively and practiced regularly but still not be easily recalled when needed. Words which are read successfully on one page may seem totally unfamiliar on the next.

Another important neurological process which underpins skilled reading and spelling is phonological awareness (the ability to perceive and manipulate sounds within words). There is strong research evidence to show that dyslexic difficulties are often due to dysfunctional phonological skills. For example, the word 'cake' may be given as a rhyme for 'cat', the word 'hospital' may be thought to contain the sounds 'h-o-d-i-p-i-l' or the sounds 'sm-e-ll' may be blended to make the word 'snail'.

Dyslexia is also associated with difficulties in rapid, automatized naming (RAN) and this may play a role in slow, hesitant oral reading. Orthographic deficits are also associated with Dyslexia and are evident in problems with recognizing and/or writing word or letter shapes.

Dyslexia often leads to problems with written expression. Poor spelling, untidy handwriting, difficulties with written expression and disjointed organization may disguise excellent understanding or knowledge.

The underlying difficulties in Dyslexia mean that despite intensive, appropriate instruction and practice progress may be slow and inconsistent. In comparison, learning difficulties caused by poor teaching, missed schooling or ill health, usually improve rapidly once appropriate teaching is provided. Lack of expected progress when appropriate and sufficient teaching has been provided is an important warning sign of Dyslexia.

The continual struggle caused by Dyslexia can have a significant impact on motivation, self-esteem and confidence.

Causes of Dyslexia

There is a strong genetic component in Dyslexia. At least 50% of students with Dyslexia have a first-degree relative with a similar disorder. In other cases, there is no obvious genetic link or cause for difficulties.

Conditions which may be mistaken for Dyslexia

Language Disorder

The characteristics of Language Disorder may overlap with those of Dyslexia and the two conditions may occur together. Difficulties with finding words and formulating sentences are typical of both disorders.

Intellectual Disability

The acquisition of literacy skills generally moves in parallel with intellectual development. Delays or disabilities in intellectual capacities will almost inevitably lead to slower than average development of reading, spelling and written language skills. A 12-year-old with a mild Intellectual Disability may be reaching their potential by reading and writing at the level of an average 8-year-old. In this situation difficulties in literacy are caused by a general impairment in learning capacity rather than a specific learning disorder.

Poor quality teaching

A student may appear to have a learning disorder, such as dyslexia, when in fact the observed literacy difficulties are simply a result of the lack of proper instruction and practice. In this circumstance the student will show rapid improvement with appropriate teaching.

Conditions which may occur alongside Dyslexia

Dyslexia with ADHD

There is known to be a significant overlap between Dyslexia and ADHD. Approximately 60% of students with ADHD will also have Dyslexia. Approximately 30% of students with Dyslexia will also have ADHD. In the classroom, there is likely to be a complex interaction between the underlying learning difficulty and a tendency to be restless and inattentive.

Dyslexia with Dyscalculia

These two conditions frequently occur together, although both can also occur in isolation from the other.

Dyslexia with Depression, anxiety, low self-esteem

The day-to-day difficulties and frustrations caused by Dyslexia can cause emotional distress and lower self-esteem.

Dyslexia with giftedness

High intelligence is usually associated with advanced literacy skills. It is not unusual for an intellectually gifted child to be reading and writing many years in advance of their chronological age. However, Dyslexia can counteract this potential for exceptional development and result in skills in reading, spelling and written language which, whilst possibly acceptable for a typical child of that age group, are a significant underachievement for the individual.

Professionals supporting the student (Dyslexia)

Teachers

Classroom teachers will modify teaching methods, curriculum materials, and assessment tasks to ensure that Dyslexia does not cause disadvantage. Special needs teachers may be involved in planning and implementing appropriate intervention.

Psychologists

Psychologists with expertise in the diagnosis of Dyslexia will provide preliminary assessment and ongoing monitoring.

Speech pathologists

Speech pathologists may work on phonological skills as well as general issues regarding reading and written language.

Counsellors and psychologists

Counsellors and psychologists may be required to offer assistance and support.

Paediatricians

Paediatricians may be involved, especially if the child or adolescent also has ADHD.

Organizations

Community organizations can offer support for the individual and training and information for teachers and parents. The International Dyslexia Association (www.inter dys.org), the British Dyslexia Association (www.bdadyslexia.org.uk), the Learning Disability Association of America (www.ldanatl.org) and the Learning Disabilities Association of Canada (www.ldac-taac.ca) are examples of such organizations.

Strategies for meeting the student's needs (Dyslexia)

Strategies for assessment and program planning

- Arrange a comprehensive assessment as a basis for planning appropriate intervention.
- Use evidence-based practices that address the identified areas of difficulty such as poor phonological awareness.

- Provide intensive, explicit instruction on the fundamentals of word decoding and encoding.
- Teach skills in the correct order so that preliminaries are mastered before more advanced skills are introduced.
- Provide intensive, individualized instruction on a regular and continuous basis.
- Recognize the need for constant repetition and consolidation of previously learned skills.
- Set timeframes for the achievement of expected learning outcomes and track progress.
- Set short, achievable goals, record and celebrate successes.
- Offer a program that is based on inclusion and equity of opportunity.
- Provide appropriate adjustments and accommodations in assessments.

Strategies for reading difficulties

- Provide modified curriculum materials. For example, modify worksheets which are at an appropriate level.
- Encourage highlighting text to help identify the key points in printed material.
- Provide the support of a reader to assist in reading curriculum or assessment materials that have not been modified.
- Use text to voice software so that documents, web pages and so on can be read automatically.

Strategies for difficulties with written language

- Allow verbal responses instead of written work.
- Encourage the use of voice recognition software to allow dictation instead of writing.
- Provide ample scaffolding, such as word lists, personal dictionaries, and so forth.
- Encourage the use of software programs that help to organize and sequence ideas.

Strategies for slow working

- Give abbreviated or modified assessment tasks so that tasks do not take an excessive amount of time.
- Adjust timeframes so that the work can be completed successfully provided reasonable effort is put in.

Recommended further reading for Dyslexia

Dyslexia: A Complete Guide for Parents and Those Who Help Them

Author: Gavin Reid
Date of publication: 2011
Publisher: John Wiley & Sons Ltd

Dyslexia and Inclusion: Classroom Approaches for Assessment, Teaching and Learning

Author: Gavin Reid

Date of publication: 2013

Publisher: Routledge

Dyslexia: An Introductory Guide, 2nd Edition

Authors: Jim Doyle and Margaret Snowling

Date of publication: 2008

Publisher: Whurr Publishers

Dyslexia Friendly Schools Good Practice Guide

Editors: Katrina Cochrane and Kate Saunders

Date of publication: 2012

Publisher: British Dyslexia Association

Take Control of Dyslexia and Other Reading Difficulties (Paperback)

Authors: Jennifer Engel Fisher and Janet Price

Date of publication: 2012

Publisher: Prufrock Press Inc

Teaching Children with Dyslexia

Author: Philomena Ott

Date of publication: 2007

Publisher: Routledge

100 with Ideas for Supporting Children with Dyslexia

Author: Gavin Reid and Sharon Green

Date of publication: 2011

Publishers: Continuum International Publishing Group

Useful websites for Dyslexia

www.bdadyslexia.org.uk
The British Dyslexia Association. Not for profit organization
Information for parents and teachers. UK

www.interdys.org
The International Dyslexia Association. Not for profit organization
Information for parents and teachers. USA

www.ldanatl.org
Learning Disabilities Association of America. Not for profit organization
Information for parents and teachers. USA

References for Dyslexia

American Psychiatric Association (2013) *Diagnostic and statistical manual of mental disorders, 5th Edition*, Washington, DC: APA.

Bell, S. (2013) 'Professional development for specialist teachers and assessors of students with literacy difficulties/ dyslexia: "to learn how to assess and support children with dyslexia"'. *Journal of Research in Special Educational Needs*, 13, pp. 104–113.

Darki, F. et al. (2012) 'Three dyslexia susceptibility genes, *DYX1C1*, *DCDC2*, and *KIAA0319*, affect temporo-parietal white matter structure', *Biological Psychiatry*, 72(8), pp. 671–676.

De Luca, M. at al. (2010) 'Letter and letter-string processing in developmental dyslexia', *Cortex*, 46(10), pp. 1272–1283.

Eklund, K.M. et al. (2013) 'Predicting reading disability: early cognitive risk and protective factors', *Dyslexia*, 19, pp. 1–10.

Fälth, L. et al. (2013) 'Computer-assisted interventions targeting reading skills of children with reading disabilities: a longitudinal study', *Dyslexia*, 19, pp. 37–53.

Georgiou, G.K. et al. (2012) 'Are auditory and visual processing deficits related to developmental dyslexia?' *Dyslexia*, 18, pp. 110–129.

Ozernov-Palchik, O. and Gaab, N. (2016) 'Tackling the "dyslexia paradox": reading brain and behaviour for early markers of developmental dyslexia', *WIREs Cognitive Science* 7, pp. 156–176.

Perez, T.M. et al. (2012) 'Evidence for a specific impairment of serial order short-term memory in dyslexic children', *Dyslexia*, 18, pp. 94–109.

Prevett, P., Bell, S. and Ralph, S. (2013) 'Dyslexia and education in the 21st century', *Journal of Research in Special Educational Needs*, 13, pp. 1–6.

Robin, L. et al. (2013) 'Subtypes of developmental dyslexia: testing the predictions of the dual-route and connectionist frameworks', *Cognition*, 26(1), pp. 20–38.

Snowling, M.J. (2013) 'Early identification and interventions for dyslexia: a contemporary view', *Journal of Research in Special Educational Needs*, 13, pp. 7–14.

Snowling, M.J. and Hulme, C. (2012) 'The nature and classification of reading disorders: a commentary on proposals for DSM-5', *Journal of Child Psychology and Psychiatry*, 53, pp. 593–607.

Thompson, P. et al. (2015) 'Developmental dyslexia: predicting individual risk', *Journal of Child Psychology and Psychiatry*, 56, pp. 976–987.

van Bergen, E. et al. (2012) 'Child and parental literacy levels within families with a history of dyslexia', *Journal of Child Psychology and Psychiatry*, 53, pp. 28–36.

Vandermosten, M. et al. (2011) 'Impairments in speech and non speech sound categorization in children with dyslexia are driven by temporal processing difficulties', *Research in Developmental Disabilities*, 32(2), pp. 593–603.

World Health Organization (2007) *ICIDH-2: International Classification of Functioning, Disability and Health – Children and Youth*, Geneva: WHO.

World Health Organization (2013) *International Classification of Diseases, 10th Edition, Clinical Modification*, Geneva: WHO.

DYSCALCULIA (SPECIFIC LEARNING DISORDER) CHECKLIST

Glynis Hannell BA (Hons) MSc Psychologist

Name of child or adolescent   Age

Each item should be checked off using the following rating scale

0   Not at all, never occurs, does not apply
1   Mild, sometimes observed, applies to some extent
2   Moderate, often observed, certainly applies
3   Severe, frequently observed, strongly applies

Poor number sense when asked to navigate a printed number line

Touch counts or searches randomly to find a target number.........................0   1   2   3
    Sample question 'Here are the numbers 0 to 50. Where is 25?

Does not use 10s to make counting easier. Counts every number................0   1   2   3
    Sample question 'Here are the numbers 0 to 50. How far is it from 10 to 30?

Difficulties with mental manipulation of the number sequence

Poor grasp of the position of numbers. Needs to count...............................0   1   2   3
    Sample question: 'Which number comes between 15 and 17?'

Poor grasp of the order of magnitude of numbers. Needs to count...............0   1   2   3
    Sample question: 'Is 21 bigger or smaller than 19?'

Poor grasp of relative position of numbers. Needs to count.........................0   1   2   3
    Sample question: 'Is 18 or 38 the closest to 20?'

Finds it difficult to skip count, counts every number in between...................0   1   2   3
    Sample question: 'Count in threes from 11 to 25'.

Poor subitizing skills

Does not recognize small quantities at a glance. Needs to count 0   1   2   3
Given two sets of items needs to count all to decide the largest set.............0   1   2   3
Cannot divide small quantities into equal halves without counting 0   1   2   3

Difficulties in understanding place value

Does not understand place value..0   1   2   3
    Sample question: 'How many 10s in 34?'

Does not use place value to multiply by 10 or 100....................................0   1   2   3
    Sample questions: 'What is 14 × 10? What is 39 × 100?'

Does not use place value to divide by 10 or 100.......................................0   1   2   3
    Sample questions: 'What is 150 ÷10?' 'What is 300 ÷100?'

Poor memory for number facts or procedures

Difficulties in learning basic number facts.....................................0   1   2   3
Forgets what to do in formal work, confuses working methods 0   1   2   3
Loses track when calculating mentally..0   1   2   3

Relies on concrete counting rather than mental calculation or recall

Uses fingers or counters for simple calculations 0   1   2   3
Makes tally marks to assist with calculation 0   1   2   3
Does not 'count on' from smaller number, counts from 1 0   1   2   3
Difficulties in using the principle of commutation 0   1   2   3
    Sample question: 'If 2 with 5 is 7, what is 7−5?'
Does not use known facts, always starts from scratch................................0   1   2   3

Slow working mathematically

Does not produce quick, automatic answers, relies on counting..................0   1   2   3
Does not know how to take short cuts, works very methodically 0   1   2   3

Poor estimating skills

Makes poor estimates in math, poor judge of expected answer...................0   1   2   3
Difficulties in estimating quantities, measurements or time 0   1   2   3

Underachievement in mathematics

Numeracy skills poorer than expected for age and ability 0   1   2   3
Poor progress in mathematics despite appropriate teaching.........................0   1   2   3
Achievements and progress do not reflect the effort put in...........................0   1   2   3

Low confidence in mathematics

Low confidence in mathematics 0   1   2   3
Avoids math where possible 0   1   2   3
Low motivation in mathematics..0   1   2   3
Gets frustrated and upset with mathematics activities...............................0   1   2   3

Positive characteristics and strengths (describe at least 3)

Important notes

This checklist can be used to help diagnose and assess Dyscalculia. However, several conditions have similar characteristics and there may a range of explanations for the observations made. Specialist assessment is necessary for a formal diagnosis.

- Supporting notes on Dyscalculia (pages 44–9)
- Guides for discussions with colleagues, parents and students (pages 184–8)

SUPPORTING NOTES ON DYSCALCULIA
Characteristics of Dyscalculia

Dyscalculia is a Specific Learning Disorder. It is marked by significant difficulties in the acquisition of concepts and skills in mathematics. These difficulties occur despite adequate instruction and normal intelligence.

Like Dyslexia, Dyscalculia is due to a dysfunction in the way in which the brain processes and retains particular forms of information. Mathematical thinking requires 'number sense' which can be described as an intuitive sense of numbers and their relationship with each other. Research shows us that particular brain structures are involved in this form of mental processing. In Dyscalculia 'number sense', understanding of mathematical concepts, ability to perform mathematical operations and overall performance in mathematics are significantly less well developed than would be expected when age, education and general intelligence are taken into consideration.

Studies show that a fundamental difficulty underpinning Dyscalculia is a poorly developed mental-spatial representation of the number line. In turn this leads to uncertainty about the order of magnitude of numbers and their position relative to each other. If number sequences are visualized correctly then it is relatively easy to 'see' that 50 is half way between 0 and 100. However, if the mental image is of a random collection of numbers in no particular order, then there is no way of knowing what relationship exists between 50 and 100.

Skilled mathematicians frequently use good estimates in place of detailed calculation. However skilled estimating depends on good number sense and the ability to use quick approximations in place of laborious mechanical calculations. Deficits in number sense and difficulties in using quick recall and 'short cut' working methods are characteristic of Dyscalculia. It follows that estimating skills will be significantly impaired.

Poor number sense can lead to a lack of awareness of fundamentals such as the composition and decomposition of numbers and the commutative principle. As an example, a child or adolescent with Dyscalculia may treat $10 - 3 = 7$ and 7 with $3 = 10$ as two, quite distinct pieces of information to be remembered. They may be unable to use the link between these facts to make other calculations quick and easy. If given the above facts and then asked *What is 10−7?* they may treat this as a new calculation without any reference to the information they already had.

Dyscalculia is also marked by poor memory for mathematical facts and procedures. Slow, inaccurate mental calculations and difficulties with problem solving are also recognized characteristics of Dyscalculia.

Causes of Dyscalculia

There is a strong hereditary link in Dyscalculia with other family members being likely to have similar difficulties. Other factors such as extreme prematurity may be implicated, but quite frequently no specific cause can be identified.

Conditions which may be mistaken for Dyscalculia

Intellectual Disability

Difficulties in grasping concepts, manipulating information and solving problems are very common characteristics of Intellectual Disability. However, in Dyscalculia these difficulties are specifically related to problems with mathematics, against a background of adequate or even exceptionally good academic and life skills in non-mathematical areas.

Poor quality teaching

A student may appear to have a learning disorder, such as Dyscalculia, when in fact the observed difficulties in mathematics are simply a result of the lack of proper instruction and practice. In this circumstance the student will show rapid improvement with appropriate teaching.

Conditions which may occur alongside Dyscalculia

Dyscalculia with ADHD

There is known to be a significant overlap between Dyscalculia and ADHD, with approximately 20% of children with ADHD also having Dyscalculia. ADHD is likely to exacerbate the learning difficulties associated with Dyscalculia.

Dyscalculia with Dyslexia

These two conditions frequently occur together, although both can also occur in isolation from the other.

Dyscalculia with Turner Syndrome

Turner Syndrome is a chromosomal disorder affecting girls. There is a very strong relationship between Turner Syndrome and Dyscalculia.

Dyscalculia with giftedness

High intelligence is usually associated with advanced mathematical skills. However, Dyscalculia can cause a specific impairment in mathematical thinking and performance, against a background of exceptionally advanced development in other areas such as language and literacy.

Professionals supporting the student (Dyscalculia)

Teachers

Classroom teachers will modify teaching methods, curriculum materials, and assessment tasks to ensure that solid progress is made with mathematical learning, despite Dyscalculia. Special needs teachers may be involved in planning and implementing an appropriate intervention.

Psychologists

Psychologists with expertise in the diagnosis of Dyscalculia will provide preliminary assessment and ongoing monitoring.

Counsellors and psychologists

Counsellors and psychologists may be required to offer assistance and support.

Paediatricians

Paediatricians may be involved, especially if the child or adolescent also has ADHD.

Organizations

Community organizations can offer support for the individual and training and information for teachers and parents:

The International Dyslexia Association (www.interdys.org)
The British Dyslexia Association (www.bdadyslexia.org.uk)
The Learning Disability Association of America (www.ldanatl.org)

Strategies for meeting the student's needs (Dyscalculia)

General strategies for Dyscalculia

- Arrange for a comprehensive assessment to identify strengths and weaknesses in mathematical skills.
- Recognize the hierarchical nature of mathematical learning. Build strong basics before introducing more advanced work.
- Provide explicit teaching in number sense, mental computation and estimating.
- Make available appropriate learning aids such as a number line or number square.

Strategies for building skills in using a number line

- Keep a number line in view and give a lot of practice in using it to assist in mathematical thinking.
- Introduce games that require counting along a number line.
- Write numerals on separate cards, the cards must then be arranged in ascending or descending order.

Strategies for teaching place value

- Use equipment such as Dienes blocks and teach the link with printed numbers (*Show me the number for these blocks. Show me the blocks for this number*).

- Work with real objects grouped into one, tens and hundreds, for example bags of buttons. Teach the link with printed numbers.

Strategies for poor memory for number facts or procedures

- Teach important number facts and practice recall over the long term.

- Provide written step-by-step guide and worked examples for procedures.

- Provide memory aids such as number charts to provide required information.

- Teach commutation to reduce the load on memory (*learn 3 × 6 = 18, then 6 × 3, 18 ÷ 6 and 18 ÷ 3 are also known*).

Recommended further reading for Dyscalculia

Dyscalculia: Action Plans for Successful Learning in Mathematics

Author: Glynis Hannell
Date of publication: 2013
Publisher: Routledge

How the Brain Learns Mathematics

Author: David Sousa
Date of publication: 2008
Publisher: Corwin Press

Mathematics Learning Difficulties, Dyslexia and Dyscalculia

Author: Steve Chinn
Date of publication: 2012
Publisher: British Dyslexia Association

More Trouble with Maths: A complete manual to identifying and diagnosing mathematical difficulties. 2nd Edition

Author: Steven Chinn
Date of publication: 2017
Publisher: Routledge

Overcoming Difficulties with Number: Supporting Dyscalculia and Students Who Struggle with Maths

Author: Ronit Bird
Date of publication: 2009
Publisher: Sage Publications

The Dyscalculia Assessment

Authors: Jane Emerson, Patricia Babtie and Brian Butterworth
Date of publication: 2010
Publisher: Continuum Publishing Corporation

The Trouble with Maths: A practical guide to helping learners with numeracy difficulties, 3rd Edition

Author: Steve Chinn
Date of publication: 2016
Publisher: Routledge

The Routledge International Handbooks of Dyscalculia and Mathematical Learning Difficulties

Editor: Steve Chinn
Date of Publication: 2015
Publisher: Routledge

Useful websites for Dyscalculia

www.bdadyslexia.org.uk
The British Dyslexia Association. Not for profit organization
Information for parents and teachers. UK

www.interdys.org
The International Dyslexia Association. Not for profit organization
Information for parents and teachers. USA

www.ldanatl.org
Learning Disabilities Association of America. Not for profit organization
Information for parents and teachers. USA

References for Dyscalculia

American Psychiatric Association (2013) *Diagnostic and statistical manual of mental disorders, 5th Edition*, Washington, DC: APA.

Brankaer, C. et al. (2014) 'Numerical magnitude processing deficits in children with mathematical difficulties are independent of intelligence', *Research in Developmental Disabilities*, 35(11), pp. 2603–2613.

Dehaene, S. (2011) *The Number Sense: How the Mind Creates Mathematics*, New York: Oxford University Press.

De Smedt, B. and Boets, B. (2010) 'Phonological processing and arithmetic fact retrieval: evidence from developmental dyslexia', *Neuropsychologia*, 48(14), pp. 3973–3981.

Devine, A. et al. (2013) 'Gender differences in developmental dyscalculia depend on diagnostic criteria', *Learning and Instruction*, 27, pp. 31–39.

Fias, W. (2016) 'Neurocognitive components of mathematical skills and dyscalculia', *Development of Mathematical Cognition*, 2, pp. 195–217.

Fuchs, L. et al. (2005) 'The prevention, identification and cognitive determinants of math difficulty', *Journal of Educational Psychology*, 97, pp. 493–513.

Geary, D. et al. (2009) 'First-grade predictors of mathematical learning disability: a latent class trajectory analysis', *Cognitive Development*, 24(4), pp. 411–429.

Kucian, K. et al. (2011) 'Mental number line training in children with developmental dyscalculia', *NeuroImage*, 57(3), pp. 782–795.

Landerl, K. et al. (2009) 'Dyslexia and dyscalculia: two learning disorders with different cognitive profiles', *Journal of Experimental Child Psychology*, 103(3), pp. 309–324.

Mazzocco, M.M.M. (2009) 'Mathematical learning disability in girls with Turner Syndrome: a challenge to defining MLD and its subtypes', *Developmental Disabilities Research Reviews*, 15, pp. 35–44.

Mussolin, C., Mejas, S. and Noel, M.P. (2010) 'Symbolic and nonsymbolic number comparison in children with and without dyscalculia', *Cognition*, 115(1), pp. 10–25.

Olsson, L. et al. (2016) 'Developmental dyscalculia: a deficit in the approximate number system or an access deficit?' *Cognitive Development*, 39, pp. 154–167.

Piazza, M. et al. (2010) 'Developmental trajectory of number acuity reveals a severe impairment in developmental dyscalculia', *Cognition*, 116(1), pp. 33–41.

Rotzer, S. et al. (2009) 'Dysfunctional neural network of spatial working memory contributes to developmental dyscalculia', *Neuropsychologia*, 47(13), pp. 2859–2865.

Shalev, R.S. (2007) 'Why is math so hard for some children?' In Berch, D.B. and Mazzocco, M.M. (Eds), *The Nature and Origins of Mathematical Learning Difficulties and Disabilities*, Baltimore, MD: Brookens Publishing.

Siegler, J.C. and Ramani, G.B. (2009) 'Playing linear board games – but not circular ones – improves low income preschoolers' numerical understanding', *Journal of Educational Psychology*, 101, pp. 545–560.

Wang, L.-C. et al. (2012) 'Cognitive inhibition in students with and without dyslexia and dyscalculia', *Research in Developmental Disabilities*, 33(5), pp. 1453–1461.

World Health Organization (2007) *ICIDH-2: International Classification of Functioning, Disability and Health – Children and Youth*, Geneva: WHO.

World Health Organization (2013) *International Classification of Diseases, 10th Edition, Clinical Modification*, Geneva: WHO.

Communication

Verbal communication depends on the development of speech and language skills. Although interconnected, speech and language are two, quite different aspects of verbal communication.

Speech refers to the ability to articulate words and the ability to maintain fluency and appropriate prosody (pitch, loudness, tempo and rhythm).

Language has meaning. It has two complementary processes; 'expressive language', which as the name suggests refers to the production of language to express meaning, and 'receptive language', which is, of course, the ability to receive and understand language spoken or written by others.

Social communication

Most children quickly learn to enjoy communicating with a range of people in a variety of settings.

In this chapter on Communication we look at two Special Educational Needs that arise when there is a problem with the development of speech, language or social communication.

SPEECH AND LANGUAGE DISORDERS CHECKLIST

Glynis Hannell BA (Hons) MSc Psychologist

Name of child or adolescent   Age

Each item should be checked off using the following rating scale

0   Not at all, never occurs, does not apply
1   Mild, sometimes observed, applies to some extent
2   Moderate, often observed, certainly applies
3   Severe, frequently observed, strongly applies

Difficulties with speech sounds

Difficulties with sounds such as 'fink/think', 'wabbit/rabbit'........................0	1	2	3
Makes a 'slushy' sound for 's'...0	1	2	3
Uses one sound instead of two, 'pade' instead of 'spade' 0	1	2	3
Simplifies sequences of sounds, 'hoptal' instead of 'hospital'......................0	1	2	3
Gets sequence of sounds muddled, 'spasgetti' 0	1	2	3

Difficulties with speech fluency

Repeats sounds, words or phrases 'I c-a-a-a-a-n do it'..................................0	1	2	3
Prolongs a sound in a word 'I mmmmmmmmade a cake'...............................0	1	2	3
Mouths a sound but cannot say it 'I ——want to go'....................................0	1	2	3

Difficulties with speech prosody and voice

Pitch of voice is too high or too low...0	1	2	3
Voice is gruff or raspy 0	1	2	3
Rate of speech is a concern, too fast or too slow......................................0	1	2	3
Volume of speech is too loud or too quiet...0	1	2	3
Voice rises and falls in an unusual way when speaking..............................0	1	2	3
Speaks in a flat monotone 0	1	2	3

Difficulties with sequence of language

Finds it hard to tell a story in sequence 0	1	2	3
Finds it hard to recite nursery rhymes, times tables, days in order...............0	1	2	3
Slow learning to count and recite the alphabet..0	1	2	3

Word-finding difficulties

Gets stuck mid-sentence, cannot find the right word...................................0	1	2	3
Uses word substitutes such as 'thingy', 'stuff,' etc. 0	1	2	3
Forgets names or words that are familiar...0	1	2	3
Slow to learn new words or names...0	1	2	3
Stilted and lacks fluency in reading 0	1	2	3

Difficulties with expressive language

Gets words mixed up, *'yesterday'* instead of *'tomorrow'*	0	1	2	3
Gets words muddled *'I was set up'* instead of *'I was upset'*	0	1	2	3
Difficulties in getting their message across	0	1	2	3
Gives up trying to explain; says 'It doesn't matter' or 'Nothing'	0	1	2	3
Uses gesture, facial expressions, and mime	0	1	2	3

Difficulties with receptive language

Suspected of having hearing difficulties even though hearing is fine	0	1	2	3
Misunderstands what is said	0	1	2	3
Does not enjoy listening to stories; prefers pictures or action	0	1	2	3
Gets confused with instructions	0	1	2	3
Inattentive when required to listen	0	1	2	3
Often does the wrong thing when instructions are given	0	1	2	3
Watches others and follows what they do	0	1	2	3
Asks others to repeat what they have said	0	1	2	3

Difficulties with social language

Poor at conversation, interrupts, changes topic, talks nonstop	0	1	2	3
Makes socially inappropriate remarks	0	1	2	3
Does not seem to understand tone of voice	0	1	2	3
Very literal; does not understand jokes, puns or metaphors	0	1	2	3
Does not use appropriate facial expression or eye contact	0	1	2	3

Not confident in using language

Reluctant to talk to unfamiliar people	0	1	2	3
Does not volunteer to speak in class	0	1	2	3
Does not like to talk on the telephone	0	1	2	3

Positive characteristics and strengths (describe at least 3)

Important notes

This checklist can be used to help diagnose and assess Speech and Language Disorders. However, several conditions have similar characteristics and there may a range of explanations for the observations made. Specialist assessment is necessary for a formal diagnosis.

- Supporting notes on Speech and Language Disorders (pages 54–61)
- Guides for discussions with colleagues, parents and students (pages 184–8)

SUPPORTING NOTES ON SPEECH AND LANGUAGE DISORDERS

Characteristics of Speech and Language Disorders

There are various sub types of Speech and Language Disorders, all of which create difficulties in verbal communication.

If the disorder is primarily related to speech, then others may find it difficult to understand what the child or adolescent is saying. If the problem is more to do with language, then there may be problems in formulating sentences or in understanding what has been said or written.

The Speech and Language Disorders checklist taps into the most notable feature of commonly occurring Speech and Language Disorders.

Speech Disorders

Speech Disorders are neuro-developmental disorders which have various clinical sub types including Childhood Apraxia of Speech. In this condition the brain has problems in planning the movements required for speech.

Another form of speech disorder is Dysarthria where there is impaired movement of the muscles used to speak, resulting in speech which may be difficult to understand.

Speech disorder may be due to difficulties in perceiving the sounds (poor phonological awareness) or due to difficulties in saying the sounds (Articulation Disorder).

Difficulties with fluency of speech are also a form of Speech Disorder. Sounds or words may be repeated, prolonged or blocked, disturbing the normal flow of speech. Speech may also be disjointed, with too many pauses and unfinished sentences.

Difficulties with pitch, loudness, tempo, and rhythm (prosody) and voice quality are also Speech Disorders.

Language Disorders

Language refers to the capacity to use and understand words when they are organized into sentences, or sequences of sentences. Language competence involves both producing and comprehending complex language.

Language has two complementary processes; 'expressive language' which as the name suggests refers to the production of language to express meaning and 'receptive language' which is, of course, the ability to receive and understand language spoken or written by others.

Language Disorders are classified as a neuro-developmental disorders. Either expressive or receptive language (or both) may be disordered in some way and overall the emergence of language may be delayed.

A disorder in expressive language is marked by difficulty acquiring new words, problems with word finding or word use, and the use of shortened sentences and simplified or disordered grammatical structures. Word order may be jumbled for example, asking 'That what?' instead of 'What's that?' There may be difficulties in structuring long sentences and in joining sentences together to form a logical sequence.

In older students an expressive Language Disorder may be most evident in written language, with poor expression, badly constructed sentences and poorly organized text.

A disorder in receptive language may lead to difficulties in understanding complex sentences. For example, when asked '*What should you do if you cut your finger?*' a student with a Language Disorder might answer something like '*Blood comes out*'. They have heard the key words 'cut' and 'finger' but have not processed the meaning of the sentence correctly.

In older students a disorder in receptive language may be evident in poor reading comprehension or problems in following verbal instruction.

Language is important in thinking and manipulating ideas. A significant delay in the development of Theory of Mind – understanding that others may think differently from oneself and each other) seems to be associated with a Language Disorder.

Causes of Speech and Language Disorders

Some children have congenital physical difficulties such as a cleft palate, cerebral palsy, cranio-facial, upper respiratory or hearing problems that are the primary disorders leading to associated problems with speech.

Motor planning difficulties leading to verbal dyspraxia can be caused by pre and peri natal problems but can also occur without an obvious cause.

A Language Disorder can also be acquired through a head injury or medical condition such as encephalitis, although these are uncommon situations.

Family history can also play its part, with Speech and Language Disorders occurring in several members of the same family. In many cases no cause can be identified.

Conditions which may be mistaken for Speech and Language Disorders

Normal development

Young children's speech and language takes time to develop and immaturities in speech and language are quite normal in the early years. A Speech or Language Disorder is suspected if the child's speech and language does not keep pace with normal developmental milestones.

Cerebral Palsy, cleft palate and other physical disabilities

Children with physical disabilities may have speech difficulties as part and parcel of their condition.

Hearing impairment

A hearing impairment may cause a disruption to speech and/or language, so it is important to make sure that hearing has been thoroughly checked as the first step in assessing any speech or language problems.

Intellectual Disability

Children or adolescents with an Intellectual Disability may appear to have a Speech or Language Disorder. However, the two conditions can be readily differentiated by the fact that in the case of an Intellectual Disability there will be additional, significant difficulties in areas such as self-care, life skills and nonverbal problem solving as well as delays or disorders in speech and language development.

Asperger Syndrome

Asperger Syndrome is characterized by stilted or somewhat stereotyped language and difficulties in maintaining a dialogue with a conversational partner. In the checklist you will see there is one section on social language; significant problems in this area would suggest that the possibility of Asperger Syndrome should also be examined.

Autism

Dysfunctional or poorly developed language is an intrinsic part of Autism.

Selective Mutism

Selective Mutism can easily be mistaken for a type of Speech or Language Disorder. The student may be unwilling to speak at all in some situations, such as school, but be quite talkative at home. There is some evidence that Selective Mutism is sometimes associated with Speech and Language Disorders

English as an alternative language (EAL)

Students who speak language(s) other than English may seem as if they have a type of Speech or Language Disorder, simply because they are inexperienced in speaking English. However, on rare occasions the student with EAL may also have a Speech or Language Disorder (which is likely to occur in all of the languages they speak).

Conditions which may occur alongside Speech and Language Disorders

Speech and Language Disorders with Dyslexia

Phonological difficulties may be evident in speech and in reading and spelling. Difficulties with expressive and/or receptive language can have an impact on literacy skills.

Speech and Language Disorders with Attention-Deficit/Hyperactivity Disorder (ADHD)

Attention-Deficit/Hyperactivity Disorder is associated with a Language Disorder to a mild degree.

Speech and Language Disorders with Developmental Coordination Disorder

Research shows that these disorders often occur concurrently.

Speech and Language Disorders with emotional or behavioural problems

It is not uncommon for Speech and Language Disorders to cause problems with social and emotional adjustment simply because of the anxieties and frustrations caused by communication difficulties. This is particularly so if social language is poorly developed.

Professionals supporting the student (Speech and Language Disorders)

Speech and language therapists

Treating Speech and Language Disorders is a specialized area and an appropriately trained speech and language therapist should be closely involved in planning and delivering an intervention program.

Strategies for meeting the student's needs (Speech and Language Disorders)

General strategies for Speech and Language Disorders

- Arrange for an assessment by a speech and language therapist if this has not already been done.
- Ensure that an individualized treatment program is in place and that home and school are using the recommended strategies.
- Respond to the message, not the way it is said.
- Don't correct or interrupt.
- Allow plenty of time for them to speak without competition from others.
- Don't finish their sentences.
- Show you have understood what they said by rephrasing what they have just said.
- Don't offer hints such as 'slow down' as this does not usually help.
- In the case of EAL ensure that an assessment looks at the student's language development across all the languages used by the student.

Strategies for receptive language difficulties

- There is a strong possibility that receptive Language Disorder will cause difficulties with learning. Provide appropriate supplementary support if this is the case.

- Continuous processing of language can be exhausting. Allow 'language-free' periods of time during the school day to provide some respite from the demands of processing and producing language.

- Ensure that information and instructions given are in short, clear sentences, with animated facial and voice expressions and practical demonstration if possible.

- Avoid long, complex verbal explanations; break information into small sections.

- Supplement verbal teaching with demonstrations, illustrations and hands-on learning.

- Reading comprehension will probably be affected by a receptive Language Disorder so consider the need for additional support and modified curriculum materials.

Strategies for expressive language difficulties

- Allow unpressured time for them to explain what they are trying to say.

- If word finding difficulties occur offer multiple choice prompts, such as 'Was it a camel or a donkey?'

- Provide questions and prompts to assist with structure. 'How did it all start? What happened next?'

- Offer alternative assessments that do not rely heavily on written or spoken language, such as a practical project in place of an essay.

- Word processing programs that predict the next word and read back what has been written can be very helpful.

- Encourage the use of the grammar check in the word processing package being used and ensure that it is appropriately customized.

Strategies for social language difficulties

- Provide coaching in social skills/social language.

- Use good role models and encourage 'watch and learn'.

- Consider looking at Asperger Syndrome if social communication difficulties seem severe.

Recommended further reading for Speech and Language Disorders

First Words: A Parent's Step-by-Step Guide to Helping a Child with Speech and Language Delays

Author: Barbara Offenbacher
Date of publication: 2013
Publisher: Rowman and Littlefield Publishers Inc

Handbook of Child Language Disorders, 2nd Edition

Editor: Richard Schartz
Date of Publication: 2017
Publisher: Psychology Press

The Handbook of Language and Speech Disorders

Editors: Jack Damico, Nicole Müller and Martin J. Ball
Date of publication: 2013
Publisher: John Wiley Ltd

Language Disorders: A Functional Approach to Assessment and Intervention, 5th Edition

Author: Robert Owens
Date of publication: 2010
Publisher: Pearson

Language Disorders from Infancy through Adolescence: Listening, Speaking, Reading, Writing, and Communicating, 5th Edition

Author: Rhea Paul
Date of publication: 2017
Publisher: Mosby

The Parent's Guide to Speech and Language Problems

Author: Debbie Feit
Date of publication: 2007
Publisher: McGraw Hill

Targeting Language Delays: IEP Goals & Activities for Students with Developmental Challenges

Author: Caroline Lee
Date of publication: 2014
Publisher: Woodbine House Inc.

Useful websites for Speech and Language Disorders

www.afasicengland.org.uk
Afasic England. Not for profit organization
Information for parents and teachers. UK

www.childdevelopmentinfo.com
Child Development Institute. Not for profit organization
Information for parents. USA

www.ldanatl.org
Learning Disabilities Association of America. Not for profit organization
Information for parents and teachers. USA

www.naplic.org.uk
National Association of Professionals concerned with Language Impairment in Children. Professional Organization
Information for teachers and therapists. UK

References for Speech and Language Disorders

American Psychiatric Association (2013) *Diagnostic and statistical manual of mental disorders, 5th Edition*, Washington, DC: APA.

Boudien, C. and Flapper, M. (2013) 'Developmental coordination disorder in children with specific language impairment: co-morbidity and impact on quality of life', *Research in Developmental Disabilities*, 34(2), pp. 756–763.

Farrar, M. (2009) 'Language and theory of mind in preschool children with specific language impairment', *Journal of Communication Disorders*, 42(6), pp. 428–441.

Martina, H. et al. (2011) 'Grammar predicts procedural learning and consolidation deficits in children with specific language impairment', *Research in Developmental Disabilities*, 32(6), pp. 2362–2375.

Natalia R. et al. (2011) 'The relationship between syntactic development and Theory of Mind: Evidence from a small-population study of a developmental language', *Journal of Neurolinguistics*, 24(4), pp. 476–496.

Parisse, C. and Maillart, C. (2009) 'Specific language impairment as systemic developmental disorders', *Journal of Neurolinguistics*, 22(2), pp. 109–122.

Quinn, M.T. (2009) 'Assessing and intervening with children with Speech and Language Disorders', in Miller. D. (Ed.), *Best Practices in School Neuropsychology: Guidelines for Effective Practice, Assessment, and Evidence-Based Intervention*, Hoboken, NJ: John Wiley & Sons, Inc.

Ricketts, J. (2011) 'Research Review: Reading comprehension in developmental disorders of language and communication', *Journal of Child Psychology and Psychiatry*, 52, pp. 1111–1123.

Trauner, D. and Nass, R. (2017) 'Developmental Language Disorders', in Swaiman, K. et al. (Eds), *Swaiman's Pediatric Neurology*, 6, pp. 431–436.

World Health Organization (2007) *ICIDH-2: International Classification of Functioning, Disability and Health – Children and Youth*, Geneva: WHO.

World Health Organization (2013) *International Classification of Diseases, 10th Edition, Clinical Modification*, Geneva: WHO.

THE SELECTIVE MUTISM CHECKLIST

Glynis Hannell BA(Hons) MSc Psychologist

Name of child or adolescent   Age

Each item should be checked off using the following rating scale

0   Not at all, never occurs, does not apply
1   Mild, sometimes observed, applies to some extent
2   Moderate, often observed, certainly applies
3   Severe, frequently observed, strongly applies

Unwillingness to speak

Reluctant to speak to anyone outside of the family home 0	1	2	3
Reluctant to speak to visitors to the family home 0	1	2	3
Willing to speak to some family members but not others 0	1	2	3
May speak to children but not adults outside of the home 0	1	2	3
Unwilling to speak if anyone is watching them...0	1	2	3
Won't answer when spoken to 0	1	2	3

Adequate language development

Does talk to close family and people they know well....................................0	1	2	3

Subtle language difficulties

Was later than average in learning to talk 0	1	2	3
Sometimes seems to have trouble expressing themselves 0	1	2	3

Use of nonverbal communication

Uses gestures, shrugs or facial expressions instead of words......................0	1	2	3
Nods or shakes head appropriately when spoken to 0	1	2	3
Points or touches instead of speaking...0	1	2	3
Uses grunts in place of words..0	1	2	3
Just stares blankly when spoken to..0	1	2	3
Won't look people in the eye 0	1	2	3

Problem lasts for more than a month

Unwilling to speak to some people for at least a month...............................0	1	2	3
Unwilling to speak in some situations for at least a month..........................0	1	2	3

Problem does not respond to pressure

Cannot be bribed into speaking 0	1	2	3
Does not respond to threats or punishments 0	1	2	3

Cautious personality

Extremely shy	0	1	2	3
Does not like to take risks of any kind	0	1	2	3
Slow to gain confidence in new situations	0	1	2	3
Joins in group singing, but stops if watched	0	1	2	3

Inflexibility

Stubborn over little things	0	1	2	3
Was slow or resistant to toilet training	0	1	2	3
Very picky about food, clothes	0	1	2	3
Often has tantrums if they cannot get their own way	0	1	2	3
Rigid about routines	0	1	2	3
Does not like change	0	1	2	3
Obsessional, excessively neat or fussy	0	1	2	3
Does not like unusual textures, tastes or physical sensations	0	1	2	3

There are no other reasons for unwillingness or inability to speak

Has been traumatized	Yes	No	Unknown
Is Autistic	Yes	No	Unknown
Has an Intellectual Disability	Yes	No	Unknown
Has a Receptive or Expressive Language Disorder	Yes	No	Unknown
Is seriously ill	Yes	No	Unknown
English is an alternative language (EAL)	Yes	No	Unknown
Has a hearing impairment	Yes	No	Unknown

Positive characteristics and strengths (describe at least 3)

Important notes

This checklist can be used to help diagnose and assess Selective Mutism. However, several conditions have similar characteristics and there may a range of explanations for the observations made. Specialist assessment is necessary for a formal diagnosis.

- Supporting notes on Selective Mutism (pages 64–9)
- Guides for discussions with colleagues, parents and students (pages 184–8)

SUPPORTING NOTES ON SELECTIVE MUTISM

Characteristics of Selective Mutism

Typically, a child with Selective Mutism will be verbally communicative at home but will fail to speak at all in a setting such as at child care, in the classroom or in a similar environment. Usually the condition only lasts a few months, but it can be protracted in some cases.

Children with Selective Mutism may communicate nonverbally by using facial expression, gestures or physical expression, such as taking people by the hand to lead them to something of interest. Sometimes the child will verbalize but use a different voice from their normal one or simply use short grunts or monosyllables.

Some children with Selective Mutism will speak outside of their home, but only to other children, when they feel that they are not observed by adults.

Generally speaking children with Selective Mutism are very resistant to deliberate attempts to make them speak. Indeed, trying to force them to speak is often counterproductive and has the reverse effect. Selective Mutism will often be at its worst when adults demand that the child speaks, if there are rewards or punishments contingent on speaking, if the child is singled out to speak or if there is an audience.

Children who display Selective Mutism are usually relatively young. The condition may appear at preschool level, when the child attends child care or kindergarten, and may continue through the early years of schooling. It is very unusual for a child older than 8 or 9 years of age to display this condition.

Causes of Selective Mutism

There is no known cause of Selective Mutism, other than it generally occurs in children who are by nature shy or anxious. There may be a family history of Anxiety Disorder.

Conditions which may be mistaken for Selective Mutism

Language Disorder

A child with a severe Language Disorder may not have the skills or confidence to answer a question or join in a conversation.

Speech Disorder

Children who have an articulation or speech difficulty may choose not to speak in situations in which they are not certain of being understood.

EAL

Children who speak more than one language may be uncomfortable using a second language with which they are less confident. This might mean they speak freely in their first language in their home environment, but are reluctant to communicate outside of the home using a second language.

Autism

Children with Autism are likely to have significantly impaired communication skills. However, they are clearly differentiated from children with Selective Mutism by the fact that their lack of communication is not selective and generally occurs across all environments.

Intellectual Disability

Children with an Intellectual Disability may have impaired communication. They may be less verbal in situations in which they feel less secure or in which the communication environment is too complex for them to process.

Anxiety Disorder

Selective Mutism is classified as a form of Anxiety Disorder.

Maltreated

Children who have been maltreated, abused or bullied may become uncommunicative, particularly when they are deeply distressed.

Conditions which may occur alongside Selective Mutism

Selective Mutism with Language Disorder

Some children with Selective Mutism may have a subtle expressive Language Disorder, which undermines their confidence in their own skills in verbal communication.

Selective Mutism with auditory processing difficulties

Difficulties in auditory processing during vocalisation may contribute to anxiety about speaking.

Selective Mutism with Anxiety Disorder

Children with Selective Mutism are more likely to have generalized anxiety, social anxiety or specific phobias or fears than other children of their age.

Selective Mutism with Obsessive-Compulsive Disorder

Obsessive-compulsive behaviour can also be associated with Selective Mutism.

Selective Mutism with behavioural difficulties

Some children who are unwilling to speak outside of the home environment are oppositional or defiant within it.

Professionals supporting the student (Selective Mutism)

Teachers and care givers

Teachers and special educators will have a role in supporting the child with Selective Mutism.

Speech and language pathologists

A speech pathologist's services will be important in supporting the child's communication skills. It will also be important to establish that the child does in fact have normal receptive and expressive language, and that there is no Language Impairment underlying the child's reluctance to speak in some settings.

Psychiatrists or psychologists

A psychiatrist or psychologist may be involved when Selective Mutism is severe or continues for an extended period of time. Medication can sometimes assist in treating the underlying anxiety.

Strategies for meeting the student's needs (Selective Mutism)

- Selective Mutism is driven by anxiety and occasionally by oppositional behaviour. Trying to force a child to speak generally has the opposite effect.

- Selective Mutism will be minimized in situations in which the child is free to choose to speak or not.

- Children are sometimes more comfortable about speaking if they do not have to make eye contact or speak to an obvious audience.

- It also helps if children can speak as softly or briefly as they like and if the fact that they are speaking is accepted without fuss or comment.

- Establish a secure and predictable routine in the preschool or school setting.

- Encourage the child to join in both physically and verbally, but do not force the issue.

- Talk to the child often, but without demanding a response.

- Children will generally speak first to an adult with whom they have developed a warm, positive rapport. Provide opportunities for the child to have a consistent adult around and allow opportunities for them to be together, without an audience.

- Many children with Selective Mutism will speak to other children, provided adults are out of hearing. Ensure that there are ample opportunities for the child with Selective Mutism to play with peers, in situations where they are apparently unobserved and not overheard.

- If the child does talk to peers but not adults, it is sometimes possible to break down the child-adult communication barrier by a trusted, familiar adult joining in with the children's group and engaging in their play. For instance, a small group of children, including the child with Selective Mutism, are sitting at a table drawing and colouring. The adult sits beside the child (making no eye contact) and joins the activity and general chatter: 'I'm doing mine blue . . . Julia, can I please have the red? . . . I think I'll do another one . . . Is that your brother?' First, only ask the child with Selective Mutism for physical responses, such as passing you a crayon that you need. Then ask a question that can quite naturally be given a nonverbal answer, such as nodding. Only then create openings for verbal answers. If the child still does not speak, do not force the issue. With time and patience, the barrier does usually come down.

- Encourage the child to communicate in any way that feels comfortable. For instance, encourage gestures, signing, the use of a communication board, or any other means of interaction.

- If possible, create a good bridge between home and school. A teacher or caregiver may visit the child at home, talking to the child's parents in a relaxed setting. The child may or may not participate verbally, but will often begin to warm to the adult, who is someone usually seen only in a school setting.

- Some children with Selective Mutism really want to participate verbally in their class, but do not have the courage to do so. They might sometimes prepare a video or an audiotape at home, which can be played to a teacher or a small group of supportive peers as their means of contributing to the verbal exchange of the classroom.

- Some children with Selective Mutism will sing, count, read out loud, or speak through a puppet even though they will not speak spontaneously. These are all useful transition activities, helping break down the barriers of anxiety and reluctance to communicate.

Recommended further reading for Selective Mutism

Can I Tell You about Selective Mutism? A Guide for Friends, Family and Professionals

Authors: Maggie Johnson, Alison Wintgens and Robyn Gallow

Date of publication: 2012

Publisher: Jessica Kingsley Publishers

Easing School Jitters for the Selectively Mute Child

Author: Elisa Shipon-Blum

Date of publication: 2012

Publisher: Selective Mutism Anxiety Research and Treatment Centre (Smart Centre)

Helping Children with Selective Mutism and Their Parents: A guide for School Based Professionals

Author: Christopher Kearney

Date of publication: 2010

Publisher: Oxford University Press

The Selective Mutism Treatment Guide: Manuals for Parents, Teachers, and Therapists: Still Waters Run Deep

Author: Ruth Perednik
Date of publication: 2011
Publisher: Oaklands

Tackling Selective Mutism: A Guide for Professionals and Parents

Author: Nigel Foreman
Date of publication: 2015
Publisher: Jessica Kingsley

Treatment for Children with Selective Mutism: An Integrative Behavioural Approach

Author: R. Lindsay Bergman
Date of publication: 2012
Publisher: Oxford University Press

Useful websites for Selective Mutism

www.selectivemutism.org
Selective Mutism Group. Not for profit organization
Information for parents and teachers. USA

www.selectivemutismfoundation.org
Selective Mutism Foundation. Not for profit organization
Information for parents and teachers. USA

References for Selective Mutism

Alyanak, B. et al. (2013) 'Parental adjustment, parenting attitudes and emotional and behavioral problems in children with Selective Mutism', *Journal of Anxiety Disorders*, 27(1), pp. 9–15.

American Psychiatric Association (2013) *Diagnostic and Statistical Manual of Mental Disorders, 5th Edition*, Washington, DC: APA.

Arie, M. et al. (2007) 'Reduced auditory processing capacity during vocalization in children with Selective Mutism', *Biological Psychiatry*, 61(3), pp. 419–421.

Busman, R. and Kirmayer, L. (2016) 'Evidence-based treatment of Selective Mutism: a comprehensive workshop', *Journal of the American Academy of Child and Adolescent Psychiatry*, 55(10), S354.

Dilberto, R. and Kearney, C. (2016) 'Anxiety and oppositional behaviour profiles among youth with Selective Mutism', *Journal of Communication Disorders*, 59, pp. 16–23.

Goodman, R. and Scott, S. (Eds) (2012) 'Selective Mutism', in *Child and Adolescent Psychiatry, 3rd Edition*, Chichester, UK: John Wiley & Sons Ltd.

Keeton, C.P. and Budinger, M.C. (2012) 'Social phobia and Selective Mutism', *Child and Adolescent Clinics of North America*, 21(3), pp. 621–641.

Kehle, T.J. et al. (2012) 'Augmented self-modeling as an intervention for Selective Mutism', *Psychology in Schools*, 49, pp. 93–103.

Nieves, M.M., Mesa, F. and Beidel, D.C. (2012) 'Selective Mutism', in Ramachandran, V.S. (Ed.), *Encyclopedia of Human Behaviour, 2nd Edition*, London: Academic Press, pp. 302–306.

Nowakowski, M.E. et al. (2009) 'Language and academic abilities in children with Selective Mutism', *Infant and Child Development*, 18(3), pp. 271–290.

Omdal, H. and Galloway, D. (2008), 'Could Selective Mutism be re-conceptualised as a specific phobia of expressive speech? An exploratory post-hoc study', *Child and Adolescent Mental Health*, 13, pp. 74–81.

Stein, M.B. et al. (2011) 'A common genetic variant in the neurexin superfamily member CNTNAP2 is associated with increased risk for Selective Mutism and social anxiety-related traits', *Biological Psychiatry*, 69(9), pp. 825–831.

Steinhausen, H.C. et al. (2006) 'A long-term outcome study of Selective Mutism in childhood', *Journal of Child Psychology and Psychiatry*, 47, pp. 751–756.

Viana, A.G., Beidel, D.C. and Rabian, B. (2009) 'Selective Mutism: a review and integration of the last 15 years', *Clinical Psychology Review*, 29(1), pp. 57–67.

World Health Organization (2007) *ICIDH-2: International Classification of Functioning, Disability and Health – Children and Youth*, Geneva: WHO.

World Health Organization (2013) *International Classification of Diseases, 10th Edition, Clinical Modification*, Geneva: WHO.

Zelinger, L. (2010) 'Understanding and generalizing communication patterns in children with Selective Mutism', in Drewes, A. and Schafer, C. (Eds), *School-Based Play Therapy, 2nd Edition*, Hoboken, NJ: John Wiley & Sons.

Developmental

The term 'Developmental Disorders' is an umbrella term, which has various accepted definitions, all indicating that the disorder is part and parcel of the child or adolescent's neurological development, determined before birth and possibly continuing through the life span. The disorders are not acquired through post birth injury or illness and are not because of learned behaviours.

Developmental disorders are neuro-developmental disorders, that is the disorder originates in the brain. This is not surprising as the brain is the central control mechanism for all aspects of life. Increasingly researchers can demonstrate how and why abnormalities in brain structures or brain functions occur and link these to particular developmental disorders. For example, there is an increasing body of research evidence on the neurological differences that can be found between ADHD and non-ADHD brains.

For the purposes of this book some developmental disorders have been placed in other sections. Readers will find Intellectual Disability in Chapter 2: Cognition and learning, and Autism and Asperger Syndrome in Chapter 5: Autism Spectrum.

In this chapter we focus on the following Developmental Disabilities:

ATTENTION-DEFICIT/HYPERACTIVITY DISORDER (ADHD) CHECKLIST

Glynis Hannell BA (Hons) MSc Psychologist

Name of child or adolescent   Age

Each item should be checked off using the following rating scale

0   Not at all, never occurs, does not apply,
1   Mild, sometimes observed, applies to some extent
2   Moderate, often observed, certainly applies
3   Severe, frequently observed, strongly applies

Physically restless

Runs or climbs when it is not appropriate to do so 0	1	2	3
Finds it hard to keep still, fidgets and fiddles when seated 0	1	2	3

Impatient

Finds it hard to wait 0	1	2	3
Does not take enough time to do things properly...........................0	1	2	3
Has a poor sense of time; thinks things take too long 0	1	2	3

Verbally impulsive

Finds it hard to keep quiet, talks too much 0	1	2	3
Speaks before thinking 0	1	2	3
Interrupts, does not wait turn in conversation 0	1	2	3
Calls out in class when it is not appropriate to do so....................0	1	2	3

Impulsive behaviour

Rushes into situations without thinking 0	1	2	3
Touches things when told not to 0	1	2	3
Works too quickly and makes silly mistakes 0	1	2	3
Pushes in, does not wait their turn...0	1	2	3
Seems sorry but does the same thing again a few minutes later 0	1	2	3
Does not wait for instructions, starts without knowing what to do................0	1	2	3

Excitable

Gets over-excited, boisterous or silly in an exciting situation 0	1	2	3
Does not know when to stop with a play fight or joke....................0	1	2	3

| Is more excitable when tired | 0 | 1 | 2 | 3 |
| Loses control quickly, has tantrums over a small upset | 0 | 1 | 2 | 3 |

Inattentive

Seems to be daydreaming or in a world of their own	0	1	2	3
Does not pay attention to instructions	0	1	2	3
Suspected of having hearing problems	0	1	2	3
Seems vague or tired most of the time	0	1	2	3
Takes a long time to complete simple tasks	0	1	2	3
Slow to respond	0	1	2	3
Makes careless mistakes, does not notice mistakes	0	1	2	3

Difficulties sustaining concentration

Does not complete set tasks, gets sidetracked	0	1	2	3
Needs constant reminders to stay on task	0	1	2	3
Loses interest in activities that need sustained effort	0	1	2	3
Loses track of the conversation going on around them	0	1	2	3
Cannot be trusted to watch out for something	0	1	2	3

Poor organization

Loses things that are needed for tasks or activities	0	1	2	3
Does not plan ahead, leaves everything until the last minute	0	1	2	3
Desk, locker, school bag and so on are always a mess	0	1	2	3
Poor judge of how much time is required for a task	0	1	2	3
Does not identify priorities, wastes time on irrelevant activities	0	1	2	3
Slow to get started on tasks, procrastinates, not organized	0	1	2	3

Positive characteristics and strengths (describe at least 3)

Important notes

This checklist can be used to help diagnose and assess ADHD. However, several conditions have similar characteristics and there may a range of explanations for the observations made. Specialist assessment is necessary for a formal diagnosis.

- Supporting notes on ADHD (pages 74–81)
- Guides for discussions with colleagues, parents and students (pages 184–8)

SUPPORTING NOTES ON ATTENTION-DEFICIT/HYPERACTIVITY DISORDER (ADHD)

Characteristics of ADHD

Children or adolescents with ADHD have a rage of difficulties which fall into three main categories:

Hyperactivity
Impulsiveness
Inattention

Some children and adolescents may be predominantly hyperactive and impulsive, others may be markedly inattentive. Others may show a mixture of all three elements of the disorder.

Hyperactive children or adolescents may find it hard to keep still. They may climb and run about far more than others of a similar age and seem as if they are 'driven by a motor'. They may find it very difficult to sit still, and constantly fidget. They may find it hard to wind down at the end of the day and take a long time to go to sleep.

Impulsive children and adolescents tend to act without thinking, they may call out in class, find it difficult to sustain concentration and often behave in an inappropriate way. They are often easily excited and may not know when to stop, for example, continuing a play fight until it gets out of hand.

Inattentive children and adolescents will have poor concentration, they may skim over details or seem to be in a daydream or 'miles away'. They may work very slowly and seldom finish work in the allotted time. In a classroom, they are less obvious than the hyperactive, impulsive type of student. However, they may still have substantial difficulties with their learning, because they fail to pay attention and have difficulties in sustaining effort.

Causes of ADHD

ADHD is classified as a neuro-developmental disorder. This means that research has clearly demonstrated that there is a biological basis for the condition. Current research has identified specific genetic markers associated with ADHD and demonstrated anomalies in the functioning of neurotransmitters such as serotonin.

This scientific research tells us that ADHD is not caused by external factors such as poor parenting, poor teaching or deliberately bad behaviour on the part of the child or adolescent.

If a child or adolescent is biologically predisposed to be active, impulsive or inattentive they will probably be more challenging for parents and teachers to manage. The child or adolescent may find it harder to self-regulate their own behaviour, than others of a similar age without the condition. However poor parenting, teaching and lack of behavioural support will undoubtedly exacerbate the condition.

It is sometimes thought that foodstuffs (high sugar intake, artificial colours, or other foods) are implicated in hyperactive, impulsive behaviour. Clinical studies show that there is seldom a scientifically proven link between food and high activity levels or impulsivity. It is therefore unlikely that a child or adolescent's hyperactivity or inattentiveness is solely due to food intolerance.

Conditions which may be mistaken for ADHD

Giftedness

An intellectually gifted child or adolescent may appear to have ADHD, when in fact they do not. Their apparent difficulties may be due to the fact that they are often bored by the slow pace and lack of challenge in a regular classroom and appear inattentive or even disruptive. They may invent diversions for extra stimulation or drift off into their own interesting inner world.

Normal developmental stage

Many children are, simply by virtue of their developmental stage, active and impulsive. Normal children placed in a situation in which expectations exceed what is appropriate for their developmental level may appear to have ADHD when they do not. This may be particularly so when young children do not have appropriate opportunities for the healthy expression of normal energy levels and playfulness.

Emotional or behavioural disturbances

Children or adolescents who are depressed or anxious may appear to have ADHD. They may be preoccupied with their sad or anxious thoughts and find it difficult to break away from these thoughts to focus on the classroom activities.

Behavioural disturbances such as Oppositional Defiant Disorder can lead to impulsive, active behaviour, although it is important to note that ADHD often accompanies behavioural disorders.

Conditions which may occur alongside ADHD

ADHD with Specific Learning Disabilities

There is a strong link between Specific Learning Disabilities such as Dyslexia and Dyscalculia and ADHD.

Approximately 50% of children or adolescents with ADHD will also have a learning disability.

ADHD with Behavioural Disturbances

Impulsive, hyperactive children or adolescents may also have behaviour disorders such as Oppositional Defiant Disorder and Conduct Disorder.

Professionals supporting the student (ADHD)

Teachers

Classroom and special needs teachers will have a primary role in working with ADHD in the school setting.

Behaviour management specialists

Behaviour management specialists may also be involved in supporting teaching staff with regard to managing inattentive and impulsive behaviour.

Paediatricians

Paediatricians may offer medical support for the student with ADHD particularly if medication is indicated.

Strategies for meeting the student's needs (ADHD)

General strategies

- Ensure that an appropriate assessment has been made to correctly diagnose ADHD and to eliminate the other possibilities such as an emotional or behavioural disorder or high intellectual ability.

- Support the parents in seeking an appropriate paediatric opinion with regard to possible medical options for management. Medical treatment (including medication) can be a valuable approach to ADHD. Advice with regard to this must be obtained from a paediatrician or neurologist.

- Consider arranging cognitive behavioural therapy to help the child or adolescent manage their own inattentive, impulsive behaviour.

- Punishments and other consequences may have little impact on impulsive or inattentive behaviour. Use positive encouragements and rewards to encourage controlled, on-task behaviour.

- Tasks that are short, goal focused and active are the most easily managed.

- Use nonverbal reminders to encourage 'on task' behaviour. Two sets of cards (one set of cards for 'well done' and the other to say' focus please') can be used and placed quietly on their desk to guide appropriate concentration.

- An incentive program can help modify behaviour, provided that the goals set are attainable and are short term. To be effective incentives must immediately follow inappropriate behaviour. For example, an agreed number of 'well done' cards (see above) might earn a reward at the next lesson break.

- Foster self-respect and self-esteem at every opportunity.

- Avoid a constant stream of reminders, criticisms and corrections. Make sure the majority of interactions are positive and supportive.

Strategies for hyperactivity and impulsiveness

- Make sure that the high energy child or adolescent does have ample opportunity to 'let off steam'.

- Whispered correction can be effective. Loud, angry reprimands tend to increase agitation and impulsiveness and reduce concentration.

- Impulsive behaviour occurs without planning or logical forethought, so it is unhelpful to ask, 'Why did you do that?' It is better to state the rule that has been broken and talk about how the problem can be resolved.

- Teach and encourage the habit of 'Stop-Think-Act'.

- Instructions *not* to do something are particularly hard to follow through. Give instructions which described required behaviour: 'Stand still for a second' or 'Look at me'.

- Avoid making parents feel that they are to blame for their children's misbehaviour in school.

- Do not expect parents to control impulsive behaviour at school by giving punishments and reprimands at home.

- If possible, keep to a steady routine which includes some quiet time when settled activities are promoted.

- Set reasonable limits and stick to them. Just because the child or adolescent has ADHD does not mean that they can do what they like. Set priorities.

- Try to ignore irritating but essentially harmless behaviours.

Strategies for inattention

- The child or adolescent with ADHD should sit near the teacher's desk, as far away from distractions as possible. Set specific classroom rules and clear guidelines about what is expected.

- Make directions clear and simple, since many children or adolescents with ADHD have difficulty processing a series of auditory commands.

- Highlight the important information in a task, and cut out confusing, irrelevant detail. Use colours, highlighter pens, and so forth to make the important details stand out.

- The use of a radio loop or similar device in the classroom may help with focusing on the teacher's voice. The teacher uses a microphone (usually a small device worn around the neck), and the child or adolescent uses headphones or a small receiver worn on the ear.

- Some children or adolescents benefit from using headphones that transmit white noise, which blocks out distracting noises.

Strategies for poor organization

- The child or adolescent with ADHD will need more reminders and more help with organizational tasks than others. Work with parents to provide a supportive network.

- Allocate specific periods of time for organizational duties, for example, five minutes at the end of the school day to sort out books for homework or for the next day.

- Children or adolescents with ADHD work best where a routine is well established.

- Avoid too many small pieces of equipment, materials, and so forth. It may be better to have one ring binder with all the necessary workbooks inserted, rather than half a dozen or so loose books that frequently get lost or damaged.

- Brainstorm with the class so that those with ADHD can see how other people tackle handling organizational tasks, for example by writing themselves reminders, planning ahead, and deliberately avoiding distractions.

- Small reminder notes written on the board can act as prompts or reminders for what has to be done.

Recommended further reading for ADHD

Attention-Deficit Hyperactivity Disorder: A Handbook for Diagnosis and Treatment, 3rd Edition

Author: Russell Barkley
Date of publication: 2006
Publisher: The Guilford Press

Attention Deficit Hyperactivity Disorder: What Can Teachers Do?

Author: Geoff Kewley
Date of publication: 2010
Publisher: David Fulton

ADHD Parenting: Parenting ADHD Children Simple Book for Parents Raising Kids with Attention Deficit Hyperactivity Disorder

Authors: Pauline Johnson and Beth Burba
Date of publication: 2012
Publishers: Pauline Johnson and Beth Burba

Commanding Attention: A Parent and Patient Guide to More ADHD Treatment

Author: Tess Messer
Date of publication: 2013
Publisher: Tess Messer

Driven to Distraction (Revised): Recognizing and Coping with Attention Deficit Disorder

Authors: Edward Hallowell and John Ratey
Date of publication: 2011
Publisher: Anchor Books

Parenting ADD/ADHD Children: The Definitive Guide for Parents Raising a Child with Attention Deficit Hyperactivity Disorder (Special Needs)

Author: Elizabeth Miles
Date of publication: 2012
Publisher: Positive Steps Publishing

Successfully Managing ADHD. A Handbook for SENCOs and Teachers

Author: Fintan O'Reagan
Date of publication: 2014
Publisher: Routledge

The ADHD Workbook for Kids: Helping Children Gain Self-Confidence, Social Skills, and Self-Control

Author: Lawrence Shapiro
Date of publication: 2010
Publisher: Instant Help Books

The Complete Guide to ADHD Nature, Diagnosis and Treatment

Authors: Katerina Maniadaki and Efhymios Kakouros
Date of publication: 2018
Publisher: Routledge

100 Questions & Answers About Attention Deficit Hyperactivity Disorder (ADHD) in Women and Girls

Author: Patricia Quinn
Date of publication: 2011
Publisher: Jones and Bartlett Learning, LLC

Useful websites for ADHD

www.addiss.co.uk
ADHD Information Services. Not for profit organization
Information for parents and teachers. UK

www.chadd.org
Children and Adults with Attention Deficit/Hyperactivity Disorder. Not for profit
Information for parents and teachers. USA

www.healthyplace.com
Healthy Place. Media organization
Information for parents. USA

www.ldonline.org
LD online. Not for profit organization
Information for parents, teachers and young people. USA

www.nami.org
National Alliance on Mental Illness. Not for profit organization
Information for parents and teachers. USA

www.primarilyinattentiveadd.com
Primarily Inattentive. Blog. USA
Information for parents and teachers

www.raisingchildren.net.au
Raising Children Network. Not for profit organization
Information for parents. Australia

www.youngminds.org.uk
Young Minds. Not for profit organization
Information for parents, teachers and young people. UK

www.ldanatl.org
Learning Disabilities Association of America. Not for profit organization
Information for parents and teachers. USA

References for ADHD

American Psychiatric Association (2013) *Diagnostic and Statistical Manual of Mental Disorders, 5th Edition*, Washington, DC: APA.

Cortese, S. (2012) 'The neurobiology and genetics of Attention Deficit/Hyperactivity Disorder(ADHD): what every clinician should know', *European Journal of Paediatric Neurology*, 16(5), pp. 422–433.

Fabiano, G. et al. (2009) 'A meta-analysis of behavioural treatment for Attention Deficit/Hyperactivity Disorder', *Clinical Psychology Review*, 29(2), pp. 129–140.

Gozal, D. and Molfese, D. (2010) *Attention Deficit Hyperactivity Disorder: From Genes to Patients*, Totowa, NJ: Humana Press Inc.

Kim, D.H. and Yoo, I.Y. (2013) 'Relationship between Attention Deficit Hyperactive Disorder symptoms and perceived parenting practices of school-age children', *Journal of Clinical Nursing*, 22, pp. 1133–1139.

Leggett, C. and Hotham, E. (2011) 'Treatment experiences of children and adolescents with Attention-Deficit/Hyperactivity Disorder', *Journal of Paediatrics and Child Health*, 47, pp. 512–517.

Moore, D.A., Russell, A.E., Arnell, S. and Ford, T.J. (2017) 'Educators' experiences of managing students with ADHD: a qualitative study', *Child: Care, Health and Development*, 43, pp. 489–498.

Nigg, J., Nikolas, M. and Burt, S.A. (2010) 'Measured gene-by-environment interaction in relation to Attention Deficit/Hyperactivity Disorder', *Journal of the American Academy of Child & Adolescent Psychiatry*, 49(9), pp. 863–873.

Riddle, M. et al. (2013) 'The preschool Attention Deficit/Hyperactivity Disorder treatment study (PATS) 6-year follow-up', *Journal of the American Academy of Child & Adolescent Psychiatry*, 52(3), pp. 264–278.

Rubia, K.(2011) '"Cool" inferior frontostriatal dysfunction in attention deficit/hyperactivity disorder versus "hot" ventromedial orbitofrontal-limbic dysfunction in conduct disorder: a review', *Biological Psychiatry*, 69(12), pp. 69–87.

Schultz, B.K., Storer, J., Watabe, Y., Sadler, J. and Evans, S.W. (2011) 'School-based treatment of Attention-Deficit/Hyperactivity Disorder', *Psychology in the School*, 48, pp. 254–262.

Sharp, S., McQuillin, A. and Gurling, H. (2009) 'Genetics of Attention Deficit Hyperactivity Disorder (ADHD)', *Neuropharmacology*, 57(7),pp.590–600.

Sonuga-Barke, E. et al. (2011) 'A functional variant of the serotonin transporter gene (*SLC6A4*) moderates impulsive choice in Attention Deficit/Hyperactivity Disorder boys and siblings', *Biological Psychiatry*, 70(3), pp. 230–236.

Vance, A., Winther, J. and Rennie, K. (2012) 'Management of Attention-Deficit/Hyperactivity Disorder: the importance of psychosocial and medication treatments', *Journal of Paediatrics and Child Health*, 48(2), pp. 33–37.

World Health Organization (2007) *ICIDH-2: International Classification of Functioning, Disability and Health – Children and Youth*, Geneva: WHO.

World Health Organization (2013) *International Classification of Diseases, 10th Edition, Clinical Modification*, Geneva: WHO.

TOURETTE SYNDROME CHECKLIST

Glynis Hannell BA (Hons) MSc Psychologist

Name of child or adolescent   Age

Each item should be checked off using the following rating scale

0   Not at all, never occurs, does not apply
1   Mild, sometimes observed, applies to some extent
2   Moderate, often observed, certainly applies
3   Severe, frequently observed, strongly applies

Vocal tics

Makes sudden, recurrent, rapid vocal noises (vocal tics)	0	1	2	3
Vocal tics resembling a cough, sniff, snort, yelp, bark, grunt	0	1	2	3
Vocal tics such as swearing, obscenities, or repetition of words	0	1	2	3
Vocal tics are involuntary and cannot be easily controlled	0	1	2	3
Vocal tics can be temporarily suppressed with effort	0	1	2	3
Is unaware that they are making unusual noises	0	1	2	3

Motor tics

Sudden recurrent minor tics such as throat clearing, blinking	0	1	2	3
Socially inappropriate tics such as tongue protrusion, grimace	0	1	2	3
Complex motor tics, squatting, twirling, retracing steps	0	1	2	3
Motor tics can be temporarily suppressed with effort	0	1	2	3
Is unaware that they are making unusual movements	0	1	2	3

Vocal or motor tics occur frequently and continuously

Tics often occur in bouts	0	1	2	3
Tics occur at random times	0	1	2	3
Tics occur many times a day	0	1	2	3
Tics occur on most days	0	1	2	3
Tics continue for months at a time	0	1	2	3
Sometimes has periods of remission	0	1	2	3

Appears during childhood or adolescence

Began having tics between 2 and 18 years of age	Yes	No	Don't Know
Started with minor symptoms such as eye blinking	Yes	No	Don't Know
Stimulant medication triggered tics	Yes	No	Don't Know

Learning difficulties

Difficulties with literacy	0	1	2	3
Difficulties with mathematics	0	1	2	3

Tics change with circumstances

Tics subdued when very interested or absorbed in an activity 0   1   2   3
Tics subdued during sleep...0   1   2   3
Tics increase or worsen when under stress...0   1   2   3

Obsessive-Compulsive symptoms

Compulsive behaviour, repetitive hand washing, re-checking 0   1   2   3
Compulsive thoughts, counting, praying, repeating words silently 0   1   2   3
Obsessional anxieties such as fear of contamination 0   1   2   3
Needs to have things in a particular order...0   1   2   3

Attention-Deficit/Hyperactivity Disorder

Behaviour is impulsive, does not stop to think 0   1   2   3
Physically restless, finds it hard to keep still...0   1   2   3
Has difficulties with organization..0   1   2   3
Is easily distracted...0   1   2   3
Poor concentration, lacks focus 0   1   2   3

Social or emotional difficulties

Embarrassed or anxious about tics 0   1   2   3
Teasing or harassment an issue at school...0   1   2   3
Tends to be anxious about minor things 0   1   2   3
Seems depressed..0   1   2   3

Positive characteristics and strengths (describe at least 3)

Important notes

This checklist can be used to help diagnose and assess Tourette Syndrome. However, several conditions have similar characteristics and there may a range of explanations for the observations made. Specialist assessment is necessary for a formal diagnosis.

- Supporting notes on Tourette Syndrome (pages 84–7)
- Guides for discussions with colleagues, parents and students (pages 184–8)

SUPPORTING NOTES FOR TOURETTE SYNDROME

Characteristics of Tourette Syndrome

Tourette Syndrome is a neuro-developmental syndrome marked by spontaneous vocal and motor tics.

Vocal tics may take the form of words (including swearing or repeating words), or the tics may be nonverbal, such as a snort, bark, or similar noise.

Motor tics are sudden minor movements such as throat clearing, touching, or tongue protrusion. Some complex motor tics involve squatting, deep knee bends, retracing steps, twirling, or similar non-purposeful movements.

The tics are involuntary. That is, they occur spontaneously and are not deliberate. However, they may be temporarily subdued when the child or adolescent is absorbed in an activity, or when extra effort is used to control them. The condition tends to improve as the child matures and approaches adulthood. However, Tourette Syndrome can continue throughout adulthood.

Tourette Syndrome usually emerges in early to middle childhood, often around 7 to 8 years of age.

The child or adolescent with Tourette Syndrome is also likely to have Obsessive-Compulsive symptoms. This may include behaviours such as repetitive hand washing, or compulsive thoughts, such as repeated mental counting.

Causes of Tourette Syndrome

Tourette Syndrome is a neurological condition, that is it is caused by abnormalities in brain function. Research shows that there is a genetic link, with a higher than average likelihood that other family members have the condition. However, it can also occur spontaneously, without any previously known family history.

Conditions which may be mistaken for Tourette Syndrome

Obsessive-Compulsive Disorder

Some children or adolescents have an Obsessive-Compulsive Disorder. They may engage in repetitive behaviours, they may need to have things in a particular order or they may be anxious about things such as germs. However, they do not generally have motor or vocal tics.

Chronic vocal or motor tics

Chronic vocal or motor tics are sometimes a problem without the criteria for a diagnosis of Tourette Syndrome being met. There is some evidence to suggest that chronic tics and Tourette Syndrome are part of the same continuum, with Tourette Syndrome being a more severe and complex a disorder.

Conditions which may occur alongside Tourette Syndrome

Tourette Syndrome with ADHD

Tourette Syndrome has a strong association with ADHD. The majority of children or adolescents with Tourette Syndrome will also have ADHD, and both conditions may need treatment.

Tourette Syndrome with Specific Learning Disabilities

Tourette Syndrome carries an increased risk of general and Specific Learning Disorders.

Tourette Syndrome with anxiety

Children and adolescents with Tourette Syndrome may be anxious in addition to having Tourette Syndrome. In addition, they become anxious because of the social implications of their condition. Anxiety and stress can increase the frequency or intensity of the vocal and motor tics. Anxiety is likely to be particularly marked when the Tourette Syndrome is mistakenly treated as a behavioural problem and not a neurological syndrome.

Tourette Syndrome with Depression

Children and adolescents with Tourette Syndrome can readily become depressed because of the impact their condition has on them and those around them. As with anxiety, this effect can be significantly exaggerated if the vocal and motor tics are misunderstood and treated as a behavioural problem and not a neurological syndrome.

Professionals supporting the student (Tourette Syndrome)

Teachers

Teachers and special educators will all have a role in supporting the student with Tourette Syndrome. This is particularly so if the student also has associated ADHD and learning disabilities.

Paediatric neurologists

A paediatric neurologist is of critical importance in managing Tourette Syndrome. Medication is now available that may be appropriate for individuals with the condition.

Counsellors

Children and adolescents with Tourette Syndrome may benefit from having the support of a counsellor who can help them work through some of the issues caused by the symptoms of the syndrome.

Strategies for meeting the student's need (Tourette Syndrome)

- Recognize that any child who presents with vocal or motor tics should be referred promptly for specialist assessment and diagnosis.
- Recognize that anxiety and stress will tend to increase the incidence of motor and vocal tics. Keep the classroom environment calm and supportive and ensure that there is an emotionally safe and comfortable learning and social environment.
- When vocal or motor tics do occur, avoid drawing attention to them. They are involuntary and spontaneous, and very difficult to control.

- Provide information and counselling for classmates so that they can understand the nature of Tourette Syndrome without prejudice.
- Promote good peer support and closely monitor peer group interactions to prevent harassment or discrimination.
- Provide appropriate educational input for any learning difficulties.
- Maintain good communication between home and school so that any minor problems are recognized quickly, before they escalate into larger problems.

Recommended further reading for Tourette Syndrome

Coping with Tourette Syndrome: A Workbook for Kids with Tic Disorders
Author: Sandra Buffolano
Date of publication: 2008
Publisher: Raincoast Books

Evidence-Based Treatment of Tourette Syndrome and Tic Disorders
Author: Doug Woods
Date of publication: 2014
Publisher: Routledge

I Can't Stop! A Story about Tourette Syndrome
Author: Holly Niner
Date of publication: 2005
Publisher: Albert Whitman & Company

Managing Tourette Syndrome: A Behavioral Intervention for Children and Adults Therapist Guide (Treatments That Work)
Authors: Douglas Wood and others
Date of publication: 2008
Publisher: OUP

Taking Tourette Syndrome to School ('Special Kids in School' Series)
Author: Tira Kreuger
Date of publication: 2002
Publisher: JayJo Books

Teaching the Tiger: A Handbook for Individuals Involved in the Education of Students with Attention Deficit Disorders, Tourette Syndrome or Obsessive-Compulsive Disorder
Authors: Marilyn Dornbush and Sheryl Pruitt
Date of publication: 1995
Publisher: Hope Press

The Tourette Syndrome & OCD Checklist: A Practical Reference for Parents and Teachers
Author: Susan Connors
Date of publication: 2011
Publisher: Jossey Bass

Tic Talk: Living with Tourette Syndrome – A 9-Year-Old Boy's Story in His Own Words
Author: Dylan Peters
Date of publication: 2007
Publisher: Little Five Star Publications Inc

Useful websites for Tourette Syndrome

www.nami.org
National Alliance on Mental Illness. Not for profit organization
Information for parents and teachers. USA

www.tsa-usa.org
National Tourette Syndrome Association. Not for profit organization
Information for parents and teachers. USA

www.tourettes-action.org.uk
Tourettes Action. Not for profit organization
Information for parents and teachers. UK

www.tourette.org.au
Tourette Syndrome Association of Australia. Not for profit organization
Information for parents and teachers. Australia

References for Tourette Syndrome

American Psychiatric Association (2013) *Diagnostic and statistical manual of mental syndromes, 5th edition*, Washington, DC: APA.

Chen, K. (2013) 'Prevalence and clinical correlates of explosive outbursts in Tourette Syndrome', *Psychiatry Research*, 205(3), pp. 269–275.

Du, J.-C. et al. (2010) 'Tourette Syndrome in children: an updated review', *Pediatrics & Neonatology*, 51(5), pp. 255–264.

Eapen, V. and Črnčec, R. (2009) 'Tourette Syndrome in children and adolescents: special considerations', *Journal of Psychosomatic Research*, 67(6), pp. 525–532.

Erenberg, G. (2005) 'The relationship between Tourette Syndrome, Attention Deficit Hyperactivity Disorder, and stimulant medication: a critical review', *Seminars in Pediatric Neurology*, 12(4), pp. 217–221.

Jankovic, J. (2011) 'Tics and Tourette Syndrome', in Albanese, A. and Jankovic, J. (Eds), *Hyperkinetic Movement Disorders: Differential Diagnosis and Treatment*, Oxford, UK: Wiley-Blackwell.

Jimenez-Shahed, J. (2009) 'Tourette Syndrome', *Neurologic Clinics*, 27(3), pp. 737–755.

Lam, K. and Coffey, B.J. (2012) 'Movement disorders: tics and Tourette's Disorder', in Klykylo, W.M. and Kay, J. (Eds), *Clinical Child Psychiatry, 3rd Edition*, Chichester, UK: John Wiley & Sons Ltd.

Morand-Beaulieu, S. et al. (2017) 'The puzzling question of inhibitory control in Tourette Syndrome', *Neuroscience & Behavioural Reviews*, 80, pp. 240–262.

O'Rourke, J.A. et al. (2009) 'The genetics of Tourette Syndrome: a review', *Journal of Psychosomatic Research*, 67(6), pp. 533–545.

Robinson, L. (2013) 'Tourette Syndrome, parenting aggravation, and the contribution of co-occurring conditions among a nationally representative sample', *Disability and Health Journal*, 6(1), pp. 26–35.

Roessner, V. et al. (2011) 'Increased putamen and callosal motor subregion in treatment-naïve boys with Tourette Syndrome indicates changes in the bihemispheric motor network', *Journal of Child Psychology and Psychiatry*, 52, pp. 306–314.

Stern, E.R., Blair, C. and Peterson, B.S. (2008) 'Inhibitory deficits in Tourette's Syndrome', *Developmental Psychobiology*, 50, pp. 9–18.

Termine, C. et al. (2016) 'Impact of co-morbid attention-deficit and hyperactivity disorder on cognitive function in male children with Tourette Syndrome', *Psychiatry Research*, 243, pp. 263–267.

World Health Organization (2007) *ICIDH-2: International Classification of Functioning, Disability and Health – Children and Youth*, Geneva: WHO.

World Health Organization (2013) *International Classification of Diseases, 10th Edition, Clinical Modification*, Geneva: WHO.

DEVELOPMENTAL COORDINATION DISORDER CHECKLIST

Glynis Hannell BA (Hons) MSc Psychologist

Name of child or adolescent   Age

Each item should be checked off using the following rating scale

0   Not at all, never occurs, does not apply
1   Mild, sometimes observed, applies to some extent
2   Moderate, often observed, certainly applies
3   Severe, frequently observed, strongly applies

Delay in physical development

Delayed physical milestones such as sitting, crawling, walking....................0   1   2   3

Delay in self-care skills

Late in learning to dress/undress 0   1   2   3
Has trouble with buttons, buckles, laces 0   1   2   3
Struggles to get arms in sleeves or legs into trousers 0   1   2   3
Gets clothes inside out or the wrong way around.......................................0   1   2   3
Slow to learn to use a knife and fork 0   1   2   3
Messy eater or drinker compared with others of the same age 0   1   2   3

Gross motor difficulties

Difficulty in mastering physical skills such as skipping or dancing.................0   1   2   3
Poor at imitating someone else's movements..0   1   2   3
Clumsy or accident prone 0   1   2   3
Looks awkward when running 0   1   2   3
Poor coordination in activities such as catching or hitting a ball...................0   1   2   3
Awkward when climbing equipment 0   1   2   3

Poor muscle tone

Difficulties in holding own weight on climbing bars 0   1   2   3
Slouches at the table; finds it hard to sit up straight 0   1   2   3
Sprawls on school desk when working..0   1   2   3
Poor posture when walking 0   1   2   3
Difficulties sitting still on the floor, moves around, shifts position 0   1   2   3
Tires easily when required to exert physical effort......................................0   1   2   3

Poor balance

Poor at balancing when, for example walking along a wall or beam 0   1   2   3
Difficulties hopping or balancing on one leg 0   1   2   3
Loses balance and falls over easily...0   1   2   3
Slow to learn to ride a bike...0   1   2   3
Finds it hard to carry liquid without spilling...0   1   2   3

Poor fine motor coordination

Difficulties using scissors...0   1   2   3
Fumbles with small items such as Lego pieces 0   1   2   3
Drops things...0   1   2   3
Accidentally breaks things 0   1   2   3
Has an abnormal pencil grip; often changes grip 0   1   2   3
Presses too hard when writing 0   1   2   3
Forms letters incorrectly; jerky 0   1   2   3
Writing is messy 0   1   2   3
Difficulties sustaining neat writing; hand gets tired quickly.........................0   1   2   3
Drawing skills immature 0   1   2   3
Messy bookwork; starts in the wrong place; has poor spacing....................0   1   2   3
Slow and/or inaccurate copying 0   1   2   3

Positive characteristics and strengths (describe at least 3)

Important notes

This checklist can be used to help diagnose and assess Developmental Coordination Disorder. However, several conditions have similar characteristics and there may a range of explanations for the observations made. Specialist assessment is necessary for a formal diagnosis.

- Supporting notes on Developmental Coordination Disorder (pages 90–4)
- Guides for discussions with colleagues, parents and students (pages 184–8)

SUPPORTING NOTES ON DEVELOPMENTAL COORDINATION DISORDER

A note about Dyspraxia and Developmental Coordination Disorder

There is common acceptance that Developmental Coordination Disorder refers to difficulties in movement and coordination that are caused by a neurological dysfunction. However, there is less agreement on the definition of Dyspraxia. There are some differences around the world as well as differences within professions about the definition and use of the term Dyspraxia.

To some professionals Dyspraxia is a very close match to Developmental Coordination Disorder and these professionals are comfortable in treating the two terms as synonymous. Other professionals see Dyspraxia as a subset or type of Developmental Coordination Disorder, referring specifically to a disorder relating to the planning and execution of complex motor activity such as gesture and speech. In this light Verbal Dyspraxia refers to difficulties with the planning and production of speech. Other interpretations of Dyspraxia extend beyond motor problems to include problems with sensory perception, social communication difficulties, hyperactivity and behaviour such as hand flapping when excited.

The checklist above is based on the definition of Developmental Coordination Disorder as provided in the American Psychiatric Association's *Diagnostic and Statistical Manual, 5th Edition*. The disorder is classified as a neuro-developmental disorder where motor development and motor performance are impaired.

Characteristics of Developmental Coordination Disorder

In Developmental Coordination Disorder the neurological systems responsible for initiating and controlling physical movement do not function as well as expected. In previous years the term 'clumsy child syndrome' might have been used to describe a child who would now be described as having 'Developmental Coordination Disorder'. Such a child will have marked delays in achieving motor milestones such as sitting and walking and acquiring skills such as catching, throwing and writing. They may also have coordination and balance problems and be generally clumsy. The disorder can persist into adolescence and adulthood.

It is important to remember that Developmental Coordination Disorder is not caused by weak muscles, which would be expected to strengthen quite readily with effort and practice.

Causes of Developmental Coordination Disorder

Good motor skills depend on effective neurological systems that formulate what movements are required and then transfer appropriate messages from the brain to the muscles. If there is an irregularity or a dysfunction in this process then clumsiness and poor coordination result. These difficulties can arise for a variety of reasons including prematurity, prenatal complications and genetic factors. In many cases there is no known cause.

Conditions which may be mistaken for Developmental Coordination Disorder

General developmental delay

A distinction should be made between children who have general developmental delay (delayed development in several major areas such as intellectual development, language development, motor development and so on) and those who have a specific delay in motor development.

Cerebral Palsy, Muscular Dystrophy, Hemiplegia and other medical conditions

There is a range of neurological and physical conditions which also cause difficulties with motor skills and coordination. Specialist assessment is always essential to make an accurate diagnosis.

Conditions which may occur alongside Developmental Coordination Disorder

Developmental Coordination Disorder with Speech Disorder

Developmental Coordination Disorder can be associated with difficulties in producing and sequencing speech sounds.

Developmental Coordination Disorder with ADHD

There is evidence that the two conditions of Developmental Coordination Disorder and ADHD often occur together.

Developmental Coordination Disorder with specific learning difficulties/memory difficulties

Studies show that memory difficulties and/or specific learning difficulties very frequently occur in tandem with Developmental Coordination Disorder.

Professionals supporting the student (Developmental Coordination Disorder)

Occupational therapists and physical therapists

Occupational therapists and physical therapists will be likely to offer appropriate intervention and treatment programs for students who are presenting with either fine or gross motor difficulties.

Teachers

Teachers will provide overall support for students with Developmental Coordination Disorder.

Paediatricians

Paediatricians are likely to be part of the original diagnostic team and may provide ongoing support and monitoring.

Strategies for meeting the student's needs (Developmental Coordination Disorder)

General strategies

- Arrange for accurate, comprehensive assessments, at regular intervals, to identify the difficulties that are interfering with learning and everyday living and to track progress.

- Check for the presence of specific learning difficulties in addition to Developmental Coordination Disorder.

- Recognize that Developmental Coordination Disorder is a neurological problem that will not be fixed by extra effort or practice.

- Provide suitable seating as an alternative to sitting on the floor. Developmental Coordination Disorder may make sitting on the floor very difficult, resulting in constant shifting around to try to find a point of balance and comfort.

Strategies for physical education and sport

- Break down skills into small parts and teach without performance pressure, before team participation is expected.

- Give explicit teaching and practice in starting positions. Allow time for the position to be adopted before teaching the following move(s).

- Provide hand over hand guidance so that the correct movement is experienced.

- Encourage 'personal best' measures of progress and achievement.

- Provide a range of equipment such as larger bats or softer balls which are easier to manipulate. Change to more challenging equipment once skills are mastered.

- Fast moving team sports require extra levels of skill and reaction speed. As an alternative provide opportunities for strength and fitness development in individual sports such as swimming, golf or rowing.

Strategies for difficulties with hand control/writing skills

- Allow extra time and plenty of rest breaks when sustained writing is essential.

- Do not penalize untidy writing, focus on content.

- Use oral assessment in place of written assessment.

- Avoid unnecessary copying. Provide copies of class notes and worksheets so that the work is already set with the minimum of writing required.

- Allow the use of photocopies, photographs, printouts and so on in place of hand-drawn materials.

- Give extra time or an abbreviated task. Allow extra time in tests and examinations.

- Give dictation, spelling, and other tests on an individual basis at a pace which matches their writing speed, so that they can keep up.

- Use a keyboard or voice activated software in place of handwriting.

- Explore the usefulness of special aids, such as a sloping writing surface and easy-to-grip pens.

- Encourage good posture when doing deskwork (feet on the floor, chair well tucked in to support the back).

Recommended further reading for Developmental Coordination Disorder

Children with Developmental Coordination Disorder

Editors: David Sugden and Mary Chambers
Date of publication: 2005
Publisher: John Wiley

Developmental Coordination Disorder and its Consequences

Editor: John Cairney
Date of publication: 2015
Publisher: University of Toronto Press

Useful websites

www.dyspraxiafoundation.org.uk
Dyspraxia Foundation. Not for profit organization
Information for parents and teachers. UK

www.dyspraxiausa.org
Dyspraxia Foundation USA. Not for profit organization
Information for parents and teachers. USA

www.movementmattersuk.org
Movement Matters. Not for profit organization
Information for parents and teachers. UK

References for Developmental Coordination Disorder

Alloway, T.P. (2007) 'Working memory, reading and mathematical skills in children with Developmental Coordination Disorder', *Journal of Experimental Child Psychology* 96(1), pp. 20–36.

American Psychiatric Association (2013) *Diagnostic and Statistical Manual of Mental Disorders, 5th Edition*, Washington, DC: APA.

Chen, I. et al. (2013) 'Everyday memory in children with Developmental Coordination Disorder', *Research in Developmental Disabilities*, 34(1), pp. 687–694.

Gibbs, J., Appleton, J. and Appleton, R. (June 2007) 'Dyspraxia or Developmental Coordination Disorder? Unravelling the enigma', *Archives of Disease in Childhood*, 92(6), pp. 534–539.

Harrowell, I. et al. (2018) 'The impact of Developmental Coordination Disorder on educational achievement in secondary school', *Research in Developmental Disabilities*, 71, pp. 223–236.

Henderson, S.E. and Henderson, L. (2003) 'Toward an understanding of developmental coordination disorder: terminological and diagnostic issues', *Neural Plasticity*, 10 (1), pp. 1–13.

Magalhães, L.C., Missiuna, C. and Wong, S. (2006) 'Terminology used in research reports of developmental coordination disorder', *Developmental Medicine & Child Neurology*, 48(11), pp. 937–941.

Pearsall-Jones, J., Piek, J. and Levy, F. (2010) 'Developmental Coordination Disorder and cerebral palsy: categories or a continuum?' *Human Movement Science*, 29(5), pp. 787–798.

Peters, J., Barnett, A. and Henderson, S. (2001) 'Clumsiness, Dyspraxia and Developmental Co-Ordination Disorder: how do health and educational professionals in the UK define the terms?' *Child Care Health and Development*, 27(5), pp. 399–412.

Pieters, S. et al. (2012) 'Mathematical problems in children with Developmental Coordination Disorder', *Research in Developmental Disabilities*, 33(4), pp. 1128–1135.

Rosenblum, S. and Regev, N. (2013) 'Timing abilities among children with developmental coordination disorder (DCD) in comparison to children with typical development', *Research in Developmental Disabilities*, 34(1), pp. 218–227.

Sinani, C., Sugden, D. and Hill, E. (2011) 'Gesture production in school vs. clinical samples of children with Developmental Coordination Disorder', *Research in Developmental Disabilities*, 32(4), pp. 1270–1282.

Summers, J., Larkin, D. and Dewey, D. (2008) 'Activities of daily living in children with Developmental Coordination Disorder: dressing, personal hygiene, and eating skills', *Human Movement Science*, 27(2), pp. 215–229.

Wagner, M. et al. (2012) 'Peer problems mediate the relationship between Developmental Coordination Disorder and behavioral problems in school-aged children', *Research in Developmental Disabilities*, 33(6), pp. 2072–2079.

World Health Organization (2007) *ICIDH-2: International Classification of Functioning, Disability and Health – Children and Youth*, Geneva: WHO.

World Health Organization (2013) *International Classification of Diseases, 10th Edition, Clinical Modification*, Geneva: WHO.

Zwicker, J. et al. (2011) 'Brain activation associated with motor skill practice in children with Developmental Coordination Disorder', *International Journal of Developmental Neuroscience*, 29(2), pp. 145–152.

Autism Spectrum Disorders

Autism has had a relatively brief history. It was first described in 1943 by Kanner, a psychiatrist and physician, who noted a pattern of unusual behaviours occurring in some children, marked by poor social interaction and obsessional, repetitive behaviour.

The condition is a developmental disorder, caused by neurological anomalies, probably present at birth, which unfold as the child develops. Autism Spectrum Disorders often encompass social, intellectual, communication, emotional and behavioral difficulties. The degree of impairment can range from mild to severe.

'The jury is still out' on whether Asperger Syndrome should be in a distinct category or seen as an integral part of a continuous spectrum of autism. There is research evidence and expert opinion to support the position that Autism and Asperger Syndrome are part of the same condition. There is also research evidence to support the view that there are neurobiological differences and contrasts in cognitive and verbal profiles between Autism and Asperger Syndrome.

Whatever the clinical and theoretical debate, there is general agreement that Autism and Asperger Syndrome do have many characteristics in common and that each individual will have their own unique pattern of strengths and difficulties.

In this book the distinction between Autism and Asperger Syndrome has been retained, placing both within *Autism Spectrum Disorder* but with two separate checklists, namely:

Autism Spectrum Disorder (Autism) *93–103*
Autism Spectrum Disorder (Asperger Syndrome) *104–12*

AUTISM SPECTRUM DISORDER (AUTISM) CHECKLIST

Glynis Hannell BA (Hons) MSc Psychologist

Name of child or adolescent   Age

Each item should be checked off using the following rating scale

0   Not at all, never occurs, does not apply
1   Mild, sometimes observed, applies to some extent
2   Moderate, often observed, certainly applies
3   Severe, frequently observed, strongly applies

Difficulties with social and emotional empathy

Does not relate well to other people...0	1	2	3
Does not seem to be aware of other people's feelings 0	1	2	3
Does not point out objects of interest to others 0	1	2	3
Does not show affection..0	1	2	3
Does not understand concepts such as 'be kind' 0	1	2	3
Misunderstands other people's behaviour or feelings 0	1	2	3

Difficulties with friendships

Seems unaware of the presence of others.....................................0	1	2	3
Has few if any friends 0	1	2	3
Does not join in play activities or games.......................................0	1	2	3
Very wary of strangers 0	1	2	3
Does not understand sharing or taking turns.................................0	1	2	3

Difficulties understanding socially appropriate behaviour

Says or does socially inappropriate things 0	1	2	3
Does not get embarrassed by social gaffes 0	1	2	3
Asks for explicit feedback, such as 'Am I being kind?' 0	1	2	3

Verbal communication difficulties

No spoken language 0	1	2	3
Delayed, unusual or disordered language 0	1	2	3
Echoes what others say 0	1	2	3
Repeats odd, meaningless words or phrases.................................0	1	2	3
Does not respond appropriately when spoken to 0	1	2	3
Repeats same conversational pattern over and over......................0	1	2	3
Takes things very literally 0	1	2	3

Nonverbal communication difficulties

Does not make eye contact 0 1 2 3
Does not use facial expression to communicate 0 1 2 3
Does not 'read' facial expression in others..............................0 1 2 3
Does not exchange social smiles...0 1 2 3
Does not enjoy cuddles, hugs, or tickles................................0 1 2 3
Odd sense of social distance; stands too close or too far away..................0 1 2 3
Cannot imitate words or actions when asked to do so 0 1 2 3
Does not play imaginatively 0 1 2 3

Unusual physical mannerisms

Repetitive movements, such as flapping or rocking 0 1 2 3
Flickers fingers close to face and watches them intently.............0 1 2 3
Walks in an odd or unusual way...0 1 2 3
Unusually sensitive to some smells, textures, tastes 0 1 2 3
Unusually insensitive to pain 0 1 2 3
Self harming behaviour such as head banging, biting, scratching.................0 1 2 3

Inflexible interests and adherence to routines

Has an obsessive interest in an unusual object 0 1 2 3
Distressed by small changes in routine 0 1 2 3
Adheres to unnecessary, meaningless routines...........................0 1 2 3
Preoccupied with parts of objects..0 1 2 3
Fascinated by spinning or flickering items................................0 1 2 3

Exceptional 'islands' of memory or skill

Extraordinary memory in limited range such as train time tables..................0 1 2 3
Exceptional technical skill in one area such as music, art............................0 1 2 3

Positive characteristics and strengths (describe at least 3)

Important notes

This checklist can be used to help diagnose and assess Autism. However, several conditions have similar characteristics and there may a range of explanations for the observations made. Specialist assessment is necessary for a formal diagnosis.

- Supporting notes on Autism Spectrum Disorder (Autism) (pages 98–103)
- Guides for discussions with colleagues, parents and students (pages 184–8)

SUPPORTING NOTES ON AUTISM SPECTRUM DISORDER (AUTISM)

Characteristics of Autism

Autism is a neuro developmental disorder. It is marked by a severe impairment in socialization and language. The condition can range from profound to mild. Children and adolescents with mild Autism are sometimes referred to as 'high functioning'.

Autism is usually characterized by significantly restricted communication skills. There may be no spoken language at all. Language may be present, but it may be disordered and unusual, including repetitive use of language (saying the same thing over and over again) or echolalia (repeating what another person has said). Turn taking in conversation is often significantly restricted.

Children and adolescents with Autism may have unusual physical mannerisms such as body rocking or hand flapping. Their general movements such as walking or running may be clumsy or poorly coordinated.

Most children and adolescents with Autism find change very difficult. They may become exceptionally distressed by small changes to routine or environment. For example, food might have to be cut in exactly the same way and served on the same dish, or be accompanied by the same words each and every mealtime.

Some children and adolescents with Autism are fascinated by spinning or flickering objects or by a particular class of objects, for example, things that open and shut, vehicles with sirens, or anything with a switch. They may also be overly absorbed by parts of an object, for example a catch on a box or the handle of a cup.

Children and adolescents with Autism have marked problems in interpersonal relationships. Eye contact may be limited, and they may find it very difficult to interact with peers or adults.

It is highly likely that Autism will be accompanied by Intellectual Disability, although there may be isolated 'islands' of exceptional skill or talent, such as an extraordinary ability to remember dates or do complex mental arithmetic.

Because Autism is generally a serious disorder, it is often recognized during the preschool years. The infant's failure to develop normal socialization and early language skills combined with the early development of unusual behaviours will often prompt parents to seek advice during the child's first few years of life.

Causes of Autism

Autism is still not completely understood, although it is clear that the condition is caused by an inherent dysfunction in brain activity. Researchers are gradually identifying the nature of the dysfunctions and their causes. Autism is usually intrinsic to the child or adolescent from birth; it can also be associated with neurological impairments associated with encephalitis, Fragile X syndrome, and other medical conditions. It is not caused by adverse social or emotional circumstances. Children with an autistic sibling have a higher than average risk of Autism.

Conditions which may be mistaken for Autism

Asperger Syndrome

Some experts do not make a distinction between Autism and Asperger Syndrome, placing them both within the category of Autism Spectrum Disorder.

However, if a distinction between Asperger Syndrome and Autism is made it usually relates to the severity of the condition and also to the development of the child or adolescent's language and cognitive skills. Children and adolescents with Autism are generally viewed as having more severe impairments in general functioning. In particular, they are usually seen as having marked impairments in their language and cognitive capacities. On the other hand, children and adolescents with Asperger Syndrome may have very well-developed language and cognitive skills and exhibit milder impairments in social and behavioural domains.

Language Disorder

Children and adolescents with severe Language Disorder may also show some traits characteristic of Autism. A severe impairment in communication (caused by a language impairment and not Autism) may also be accompanied by poor socialization, resistance to change, and some obsessional behaviours.

Childhood Disintegrative Disorder and Rett's Disorder

These conditions are marked by normal development in the early months or years of life followed by deterioration in functioning, when autistic-like features begin to emerge after a period of normal development.

Conditions which may occur alongside Autism

Autism is a complex disorder which, in itself, has many facets. The child or adolescent with Autism may have marked problems with concentration, may be poorly coordinated, may show strong signs of anxiety, and will almost inevitably have learning difficulties. Generally speaking, all of these difficulties come under the umbrella of the condition we know as Autism.

Autism with Intellectual Disability

Intellectual disability is strongly associated with Autism. It is estimated that 75% of children and adolescents with Autism also have an Intellectual Disability. The correct diagnosis can only be made after expert clinical assessment.

Professionals supporting the student (Autism)

Multidisciplinary team

Autism is generally a complex, severe disorder which, generally speaking, requires intensive, ongoing input from a multidisciplinary team. Therapy (behavioural, speech, occupational) does produce observable gains, with rate of advancement related to IQ. Children and adolescents with less severe intellectual impairment tend to make better progress than those with more marked intellectual disabilities.

Teachers

In the school setting, the child or adolescent will, in most cases, have a high need for specialist input. In a general class, the child or adolescent may need a teacher's aide to help interpret the teacher's instructions, modify tasks, and give the child or adolescent support both academically and socially.

It is highly likely that the child or adolescent with Autism will require intensive individual or small group support with a special educator. Obviously, this will vary according to the particular child or adolescent's needs. A differentiated curriculum and individualized teaching will, in most cases, be essential.

Speech and language therapists

Speech therapists may be involved in supporting the development of play and communication skills. This may include support for symbolic and imaginative play, training in the use of signing or communication devices, and of course, the development of oral communication (listening and responding).

Behaviour management specialists

A psychiatrist, psychologist or teacher with special expertise in behaviour management may support teachers and parents in managing the child or adolescent with Autism, with the goal of increasing socialization skills and decreasing the incidence and severity of inappropriate behaviours.

Paediatricians

A paediatrician will generally be involved to support the overall medical input for the child or adolescent with Autism and to monitor general health functions.

Social workers

A social worker may be involved to support parents, siblings, and peers of the child or adolescent with Autism

Strategies for meeting the student's needs (Autism)

- Ensure that a multidisciplinary team is set up, so that expertise from various professional fields can be brought together. Specialist therapy (behavioural, speech, occupational) will support the classroom and special education teachers' efforts.

- Provide evidence-based information on appropriate treatments to assist parents in evaluating options for their child.

- The handout *Trustworthy or not?* on page 182 of this book can be photocopied and given to parents to help them investigate the claims of anyone offering treatment or therapy for their child.

- It is often appropriate to appoint one person in the multi-disciplinary team as the family's contact person. This means that all communication is filtered through that person, so that the family has one person to deal with, rather than several.

- Autism is a broad-based disorder, so social and emotional needs must be considered in addition to educational special needs.

- Provide intervention, support and instruction in social skills across a range of situations (classroom, schoolyard, community and family).

- Most children and adolescents with Autism have difficulties with shifts in routine or with unexpected events. Arrange the learning environment so that there is as much security, predictability, and consistency as possible.

- Introduce changes in staffing or physical location in small, incremental steps. Arrange early visits to a new classroom well before the child or adolescent has to attend school in that classroom on a full-time basis.

- Talk to parents and caregivers to establish the child or adolescent's particular idiosyncrasies with regard to things or events that may alarm, upset or delight the child or adolescent.

- Ensure that there is sufficient social support for the child or adolescent, especially when the child or adolescent is integrated with a group of peers, such as in a general classroom or schoolyard.

- At recreation times, it may be appropriate to set up a small play area where the child or adolescent with Autism may play with other, invited children and where there is adult supervision, support, and facilitation.

- Ensure that the child or adolescent's program includes as much life skills experience as possible. Becoming familiar with the outside environment, using public transportation, visiting public places, accessing community facilities, and being able to participate in normal community activities will be an important part of the child or adolescent's overall personal development.

- If necessary, consider offering respite care to the family of the child or adolescent with Autism, in recognition of the high demands that such a child may place on the family unit.

Recommended further reading for Autism

Autism: A Practical Guide for Parents

Author: Alan Yau

Date of publication: 2012

Publisher: Alan Yau

Autism Spectrum Disorders: What Every Parent Needs to Know

Authors: Alan Rosenblatt and Paul Carbone

Date of publication: 2012

Publisher: American Academy of Pediatrics

Autism: A Very Short Introduction

Author: Uta Frith

Date of publication: 2010

Publisher: OUP

Supporting Social Inclusion for Students with Autism Spectrum Disorders

Author: Cathy Little

Date of publication: 2017

Publisher: Routledge

Ten Things Every Child with Autism Wishes You Knew

Authors: Ellen Notbohm and Veronica Zysk
Date of publication: 2012
Publisher: Future Horizons

1001 Great Ideas for Teaching and Raising Children with Autism or Asperger's, (Revised and Expanded 2nd Edition)

Authors: Ellen Notbohm, Veronica Zysk and Temple Grandin
Date of publication: 2010
Publisher: Future Horizons

Useful websites for Autism

www.autismnow.org
Autism Now. Not for profit organization
Information for parents and teachers. USA

www.Autism-society.org
Autism Society. Not for profit organization
Information for parents and teachers. USA

www.Autismspectrum.org.au
Autism Spectrum Australia. Not for profit organization
Information for parents and teachers. Australia

www.nami.org
National Alliance on Mental Illness. Not for profit organization
Information for parents and teachers. USA

www.Autism.org.uk
National Autistic Society. Not for profit organization
Information for parents and teachers. UK

www. raisingchildren.net.au
Raising Children Network. Not for profit organization
Information for parents. Australia

www.usAutism.org
US Autism and Asperger Association. Not for profit organization
Information for parents and teachers. USA

www.youngminds.org.uk
Young Minds. Not for profit organization
Information for young people with Asperger's Syndrome and Autism, parents and teachers. UK

References for Autism

American Psychiatric Association (2013) *Diagnostic and statistical manual of mental disorders, 5th Edition*, Washington, DC: APA.

Balconi, M., Amenta, S. and Ferrari, C.(2012) 'Emotional decoding in facial expression, scripts and videos: a comparison between normal, autistic and Asperger children', *Research in Autism Spectrum Disorders*, 6(1), pp. 193–203.

Betancur, C. (2011) 'Etiological heterogeneity in Autism Spectrum Disorders: more than 100 genetic and genomic disorders and still counting', *Brain Research*, 1380, pp. 42–77.

Chen, M.-H. et al. (2013) 'Comorbidity of allergic and autoimmune diseases in patients with Autism Spectrum Disorder: a nationwide population-based study', *Research in Autism Spectrum Disorders*, 7(5), pp. 205–212.

Flynn, L. and Healy, O. (2012) 'A review of treatments for deficits in social skills and self-help skills in Autism Spectrum Disorder', *Research in Autism Spectrum Disorders*, 6(1), pp. 431–441.

Kaland, N. (2011) 'Brief report: should Asperger Syndrome be excluded from the forthcoming DSM-V?' *Research in Autism Spectrum Disorders*, 5(3), pp. 984–989.

Lang, R. et al. (2011) 'Use of school recess time in the education and treatment of children with Autism Spectrum Disorders: a systematic review', *Research in Autism Spectrum Disorders*, 5(4), pp. 1296–1305.

Leonard, H. et al. (2010) 'Unpacking the complex nature of the Autism epidemic', *Research in Autism Spectrum Disorders*, 4(4), pp. 548–554.

Matson, J.L. et al. (2013) 'Why are there so many unsubstantiated treatments in Autism?' *Research in Autism Spectrum Disorders*, 7(3), pp. 466–474.

McPartland, J.C. and Volkmar, F.R. (2013) 'Asperger Syndrome and its relationships to Autism', in *The Neuroscience of Autism Spectrum Disorders*, Buxbaum, J.D. and Hof, P.R. (Eds), *The Neuroscience of Autism Spectrum Disorders*, Oxford, UK: Academic Press.

Miller, V.A. et al. (2012) 'Factors related to parents' choices of treatments for their children with Autism Spectrum Disorders', *Research in Autism Spectrum Disorders*, 6(11), pp. 87–95.

Volkmar, F.R. and Klin, A. (2000) Asperger's disorder and higher functioning Autism: Same or different? *International Review of Research in Mental Retardation*, 23, pp. 83–110.

World Health Organization (2007) *ICIDH-2: International Classification of Functioning, Disability and Health – Children and Youth*, Geneva: WHO.

World Health Organization (2013) *International Classification of Diseases, 10th Edition, Clinical Modification*, Geneva: WHO.

Yates, K. and Le Couteur, A. (2013) 'Diagnosing Autism', *Paediatrics and Child Health*, 23(1), pp. 5–10.

AUTISM SPECTRUM DISORDER (ASPERGER SYNDROME) CHECKLIST

Glynis Hannell BA (Hons) MSc Psychologist

Name of child or adolescent   Age

Each item should be checked off using the following rating scale

0   Not at all, never occurs, does not apply
1   Mild, sometimes observed, applies to some extent
2   Moderate, often observed, certainly applies
3   Severe, frequently observed, strongly applies

Poor social skills

Few if any friends, chooses solitary activities 0	1	2	3
Socially inappropriate behaviour or comments 0	1	2	3
Unaware or disinterested in peer group pressure 0	1	2	3
Tries to make friends but is socially clumsy 0	1	2	3
Does not seek to share interests with others...0	1	2	3

Inflexible

Does not enjoy new experiences, unsettled by change...............................0	1	2	3
Rigid, finds it hard to meet others half way 0	1	2	3
Insists on sticking to routines that are unnecessary 0	1	2	3
Likes things in a certain order (for example toys in order of size).................0	1	2	3

Limited emotional understanding and unusual emotions

Poor insight into how others feel..0	1	2	3
Needs explicit feedback about how others feel..0	1	2	3
Expressionless when strong emotion is called for..0	1	2	3
Very emotional over small issues 0	1	2	3

Egocentric

Only sees things from their own point of view...0	1	2	3
Expects others to read their mind 0	1	2	3

Difficulties with nonverbal communication

Poor eye contact (too little or too much) 0	1	2	3
Poor judge of social distance (stands too close or far away).........................0	1	2	3
'Wooden' when cuddled 0	1	2	3
Finds it very difficult to mime or to mimic others 0	1	2	3

Restricted interests

Intense interest in a single topic such as trains or maps 0   1   2   3
Fascinated by data such as timetables, dates or scores.........................0   1   2   3
Preoccupied by parts of objects or how things work 0   1   2   3
Obsessed by a particular book or computer game 0   1   2   3

Unusual language

Very pedantic, 'speaks like a professor' 0   1   2   3
Odd accent, sounds 'foreign' 0   1   2   3
Unusual intonation, sounds 'flat' and expressionless 0   1   2   3
Speaks too loudly 0   1   2   3
Talks regardless of whether listener seems interested or not......................0   1   2   3
Idiosyncratic patterns of speech, uses unusual phrases 0   1   2   3
Repetitive speech, uses the same phrases over and over...........................0   1   2   3
Takes things very literally. Does not understand jokes or metaphors............0   1   2   3

Unusual sensory awareness

Unusually sensitive to textures of clothes or food......................................0   1   2   3
Unusually sensitive to smells or noises 0   1   2   3

Unusual physical mannerisms

Flaps or twirls hands..0   1   2   3
Unusual gait, stiff legs or exaggerated arm movements 0   1   2   3
Runs in a set pattern such as circles or a particular route..........................0   1   2   3
Runs on the spot or twirls 0   1   2   3

Positive characteristics and strengths (describe at least 3)

Important notes

This checklist can be used to help diagnose and assess Asperger Syndrome. However, several conditions have similar characteristics and there may a range of explanations for the observations made. Specialist assessment is necessary for a formal diagnosis.

- Supporting notes on Autism Spectrum Disorder (Asperger Syndrome) (pages 106–112)
- Guides for discussions with colleagues, parents and students (pages 184–8)

SUPPORTING NOTES ON AUTISM SPECTRUM DISORDER (ASPERGER SYNDROME)

Characteristics of Asperger Syndrome

As discussed in the introduction to this chapter there is robust professional debate about whether Asperger Syndrome is a 'standalone' disorder within the Autism spectrum or whether it is just as easily described as 'Autism' or 'high functioning Autism'.

Whatever professional stance is taken it is clear that there are some recognizable patterns of behaviour which are often referred to as 'Asperger Syndrome', both within the scientific literature and also the general population.

Asperger Syndrome is characterized by difficulties with socialization, behavioural and emotional inflexibility and obsessional interests, but often within the context of normal (and sometimes high or very high) intellectual ability. 'Eccentricity' might sum up many of the observed behaviours.

Adequate or even good language skills are commonly found in children and adolescents with Asperger Syndrome. Vocabulary may be exceptionally advanced. However, there are also some characteristic anomalies such as overly formal language, peculiar turns of phrase, an unexplained 'foreign' accent or an unusually 'flat' or loud voice. The child or adolescent with Asperger Syndrome may be able to deliver a long and well- informed monologue but find it surprisingly difficult to hold a conversation, take turns and respond appropriately to a conversational partner. Understanding of language may be very literal and inferences, sarcasm, humour or subtle nuances of meaning may not be well understood.

Socialization difficulties are evident in the way in which the child or adolescent fails to 'read' nonverbal or implicit messages and may be socially clumsy or inept.

'Theory of Mind' refers to the ability to understand your own thinking (for example making a distinction between knowing and guessing) and understanding that other people may think, perceive or believe in different ways. Children and adolescents with Asperger Syndrome typically have poorly developed Theory of Mind, which in turn leads to difficulties in socialization and emotional adjustment. For example, if the child with Asperger Syndrome is unable to perceive how or why a classmate might be upset, they will have limited capacity to give an empathetic and appropriate response.

Causes of Asperger Syndrome

There is a genetic link in Asperger Syndrome, with family members more likely to show similar characteristics than the general population. The causes are not yet fully understood, although current research demonstrates anomalies in the structure and function of specific areas of the brain in all Autism Spectrum Disorders including Autism Spectrum Disorder (Asperger Syndrome).

Conditions which may be mistaken for Asperger Syndrome

Autism and Asperger Syndrome are both in the Autism spectrum and not all authorities separate the spectrum into separate disorders. Some authorities believe that Asperger Syndrome is characterized by adequate, and sometimes even excellent language skills, and milder, more subtle socialization difficulties than might be observed in a child or adolescent with Autism.

Language impairment

Children and adolescents with language impairment can also show characteristics of Asperger Syndrome, particularly in the difficulties they experience in communication and socialization. Some children or adolescents with severe language impairment may show some obsessional behaviours. Expert assessment is required to make this differential diagnosis.

Anxiety Disorder

Children or adolescents with anxiety disorders may have obsessional behaviours such as repetitive hand washing.

Conditions which may occur alongside Asperger Syndrome

Asperger Syndrome with giftedness

Some children and adolescents with Asperger Syndrome are also intellectually gifted. It can be difficult to distinguish between the in–depth interest in a topic shown by an intellectually gifted child or adolescent and the obsessional interest shown by a child or adolescent with Asperger Syndrome.

Asperger Syndrome with Anxiety

Many children and adolescents with Asperger Syndrome also have clinically high levels of anxiety and may be diagnosed with Anxiety Disorder. A child or adolescent with Asperger Syndrome is inflexible and finds change difficult. They may readily become very anxious about minor changes that would not worry another child or adolescent at all, such as the prospect of a school camp, the presence of a relief teacher, or change in the way in which the classroom or school timetable is arranged.

Asperger Syndrome with ADHD

Many children and adolescents with Asperger Syndrome also have ADHD.

Asperger Syndrome with Developmental Coordination Disorder

Children and adolescents with Asperger Syndrome quite frequently have problems with perceptual reasoning. This may be associated with Developmental Coordination Disorders or Dyspraxia. This may mean that the child or adolescent with Asperger Syndrome copes with the verbal or intellectual demands of a task quite well but fails to present written work or graphics to the same standard.

Asperger Syndrome with Oppositional Defiant Disorder

The characteristics of Asperger Syndrome (inflexible, difficulties with interpersonal relationships) will readily contribute to behavioural problems. The child or adolescent with Asperger Syndrome may often appear oppositional or defiant because of communication problems or inflexibility. This is likely to be much more marked if adults do not recognize the behaviour as symptomatic of Asperger Syndrome and fail to adapt teaching and behaviour management strategies accordingly.

Asperger Syndrome with Depression

Children and adolescents with Asperger Syndrome can readily become depressed, particularly as they are likely to experience ongoing difficulties with socialization. The child or adolescent with Asperger Syndrome may lack the skills to establish stable, positive relationships with peers and can easily become the victim of teasing and harassment.

Professionals supporting the student (Asperger Syndrome)

Teachers

In most cases the classroom teacher will have primary responsibility for the child or adolescent's day-to-day support and management. Special educators may work with associated learning difficulties and may be part of the team that supports the child or adolescent with socialization.

Behaviour management specialists

Specialist support from a psychologist, psychiatrist, counsellor or behaviour management specialist may be needed to assist the child or adolescent with anxiety, obsessional behaviour and socialization skills.

Strategies for meeting the student's needs (Asperger Syndrome)

- The child or adolescent with Asperger Syndrome may have particular, idiosyncratic preferences or anxieties. Teachers and parent will need to communicate well to ensure that these special needs are understood and accommodated to avoid unnecessary distress.

- Children or adolescents with Asperger Syndrome are more comfortable when there is continuity, predictability and security. They are generally much less comfortable in open-ended or unpredictable situations. Their classroom environment therefore needs to be one that has a steady, explicit routine.

- The child or adolescent with Asperger Syndrome will need good preparation when the inevitable transitions in life occur. For instance, changing from one grade level to another, working with a new teacher, or changing classrooms will all need to be handled sensitively so that the child or adolescent has time to acclimatize.

- Cognitive Behavioural Therapy (CBT) is an evidence-based treatment for emotional disturbances such as anxiety and anger that may accompany Asperger Syndrome.

- Sarcasm, satire, and jokes may be taken literally, and this can cause great distress. Teachers therefore need to be very sensitive to how the child or adolescent perceives what is said. Clear, factual statements are the most easily understood. Explanations are often needed when a joke or sarcasm has caused a misunderstanding.

- Social situations may need to be explained to compensate for Theory of Mind difficulties which lead to poor insight into the underlying motivations and thoughts of others.

- Children or adolescents with Asperger Syndrome often need explicit social skills teaching. Other children may intuitively understand appropriate social distance, how to make friends, or how to respond to a visitor. The child or adolescent with Asperger Syndrome may need to be taught these things explicitly and to be given guided practice and coaching in real-life situations.

- Instead of being able to judge someone's mood by body language and tone of voice, the child or adolescent with Asperger Syndrome may need to be told such things as 'I am very angry about this', or 'Sally is looking very sad, so please be kind to her'.

- The child or adolescent may need explicit teaching about nonverbal communication to help them interpret facial expression, tone of voice, and other nonverbal behaviours.

- Many children or adolescents with Asperger Syndrome have excellent oral language but poor fine motor and perceptual skills. They may need additional teaching or adjustments and accommodations to take account of their problems with neatness, coordination, bookwork, and so forth.

Recommended further reading for Asperger Syndrome

Asperger's Answer Book: The Top 275 Questions Parents Ask

Author: Susan Ashley
Date of publication: 2006
Publisher: Sourcebooks

Asperger's Rules! How to Make Sense of School and Friends

Author: Blythe Grossberg
Date of publication: 2012
Publisher: Magination Press

Asperger Syndrome A Practical Guide for Teachers, 2nd Edition

Authors: Val Cumine, Julia Dunlop and Gill Stevenson
Date of publication: 2010
Publisher: Routledge

Asperger Syndrome and Anxiety

Author: Nick Dublin
Date of publication: 2009
Publisher: Athenaeum Press

The Asperkid's (Secret) Book of Social Rules: The Handbook of Not-So-Obvious Social Guidelines for Tweens and Teens with Asperger Syndrome

Author: Jennifer Cook O'Toole
Date of publication: 2012
Publisher: Jessica Kingsley Publishers

Supporting Social Inclusion for Students with Autism Spectrum Disorders

Author: Cathy Little
Date of publication: 2017
Publisher: Routledge

The Complete Guide to Asperger's Syndrome

Author: Tony Attwood
Date of publication: 2008
Publisher: Athenaeum Press

1001 Great Ideas for Teaching and Raising Children with Autism or Asperger's (Revised and Expanded 2nd Edition)

Authors: Ellen Notbohm, Veronica Zysk and Temple Grandin
Date of publication: 2010
Publisher: Future Horizons

Useful websites for Asperger Syndrome

www.autismnow.org
Autism Now. Not for profit organization
Information for parents and teachers. USA

www.autism-society.org
Autism Society. Not for profit organization
Information for parents and teachers. USA

www.autismspectrum.org.au
Autism Spectrum Australia. Not for profit organization
Information for parents and teachers. Australia

www.nami.org
National Alliance on Mental Illness. Not for profit organization
Information for parents and teachers. USA

www.autism.org.uk
National Autistic Society. Not for profit organization
Information for parents and teachers. UK

www. raisingchildren.net.au
Raising Children Network. Not for profit organization
Information for parents. Australia

www.usautism.org
US Autism and Asperger Association. Not for profit organization
Information for parents and teachers. USA

www.youngminds.org.uk
Young Minds. Not for profit organization
Information for young people with Asperger Syndrome and Autism, parents and teachers. UK

References for Asperger Syndrome

American Psychiatric Association (2013) *Diagnostic and statistical manual of mental disorders, 5th Edition*, Washington, DC: APA.

Clark, A. et al. (2016) 'EEG activity in children with Asperger's Syndrome', *Clinical Neurophysiology*, 127(1), pp. 442–451.

Gillis, J., Sevlever, M. and Roth, M. (2012) 'Asperger's Syndrome and Nonverbal Learning Disorder', in Ramachandran, V.S. (Ed.), *Encyclopedia of Human Behaviour, 2nd Edition*, pp. 199–203, London: Academic Press.

Kaland, N., Mortensen, E.L. and Smith L. (2011) 'Social communication impairments in children and adolescents with Asperger Syndrome: slow response time and the impact of prompting', *Research in Autism Spectrum Disorders*, 5(3), pp. 1129–1137.

Kloppers, F. et al. (2017) 'A cluster analysis exploration of Autism Spectrum Disorder subgroups in children without intellectual disability', *Research in Autism Spectrum Disorders*, 36, pp. 66–78.

Le Sourn-Bissaoui, S. et al. (2011) 'Ambiguity detection in adolescents with Asperger Syndrome: is central coherence or theory of mind impaired?' *Research in Autism Spectrum Disorders*, 5(1), pp. 648–656.

McCrimmon, A.W. et al. (2012) 'Executive functions in Asperger's syndrome: an empirical investigation of verbal and nonverbal skills', *Research in Autism Spectrum Disorders*, 6(1), pp. 224–233.

McPartland, J.C. and Volkmar, F.R. (2013) 'Asperger Syndrome and its relationships to Autism', in Buxbaum J.D. and Hof, P.R. (Eds), *The Neuroscience of Autism Spectrum Disorders*, Oxford, UK: Academic Press.

Stothers, M.E. and Oram Cardy, J. (2012) 'Oral language impairments in developmental disorders characterized by language strengths: a comparison of Asperger Syndrome and nonverbal learning disabilities', *Research in Autism Spectrum Disorders*, 6(1), pp. 519–534.

Tani, M. et al. (2012) 'Mental and behavioural symptoms of persons with Asperger's Syndrome: relationships with social isolation and handicaps', *Research in Autism Spectrum Disorders*, 6(2), pp. 907–912.

Torralva, T. et al. (2013) 'Impaired theory of mind but intact decision-making in Asperger Syndrome: implications for the relationship between these cognitive domains', *Psychiatry Research*, 205(3), pp. 282–284.

Volkmar, F.R. and Klin, A. (2000) 'Asperger's disorder and higher functioning Autism: same or different?' *International Review of Research in Mental Retardation*, 23, pp. 83–110.

Whitehouse, A. et al. (2009) 'Friendship, loneliness and depression in adolescents with Asperger Syndrome', *Journal of Adolescence*, 32(2), pp. 309–322.

World Health Organization (2007) *ICIDH-2: International Classification of Functioning, Disability and Health – Children and Youth*, Geneva: WHO.

World Health Organization (2013) *International Classification of Diseases, 10th Edition, Clinical Modification*, Geneva: WHO.

Social, emotional and mental health

Some children are born with a biological predisposition to anxiety, Depression or other mental health issues. Other children may have innate difficulties with self-regulation, social perception or social skills. The child's inbuilt psychological make-up will shape how easy (or difficult) it will be for them to adjust to the normal ups and downs of life.

But the child's development will not occur in a vacuum. There will be a complex interplay between the child's underlying makeup and the environment in which they develop. An adverse social and emotional environment may make matters much worse. Factors such as inadequate parenting, maltreatment, physical and/or emotional deprivation, negative role models and so on may well exacerbate a natural vulnerability to mental health, emotional or behavioural problems. Maltreatment may well create a social, emotional or mental health problem where none would otherwise have existed. Conversely a positive environment might help to mitigate some (but not necessarily all) of the potential difficulties.

This chapter contains seven checklists for social, emotional or mental health special needs. The first four items in the chapter relate to clinically recognized conditions. The remaining items cover non-clinical conditions that may still indicate that the student has special needs.

ANXIETY DISORDER CHECKLIST

Glynis Hannell BA (Hons) MSc Psychologist

Name of child or adolescent   Age

Each item should be checked off using the following rating scale

0   Not at all, never occurs, does not apply
1   Mild, sometimes observed, applies to some extent
2   Moderate, often observed, certainly applies
3   Severe, frequently observed, strongly applies

Disturbed sleep

Has difficulties getting to sleep..0	1	2	3
Restless and anxious during the night.......................................0	1	2	3
Has nightmares or night terrors...0	1	2	3

Afraid of new experiences

Wants to do something new but panics at the last minute 0	1	2	3
Worries too much before a new experience................................0	1	2	3
Won't try new things, panics if forced 0	1	2	3
Gets very worried about going back to school after a break..........0	1	2	3
Needs a lot help from adults to cope with new experiences 0	1	2	3
Hides or locks self away to avoid new experiences.....................0	1	2	3
Won't try unfamiliar food, panics if forced to try 0	1	2	3

Has physical signs of anxiety

Has nervous blink, twitch, or other mannerism...........................0	1	2	3
Gets sweaty palms when anxious..0	1	2	3
Goes pale under pressure 0	1	2	3
Stomach pain or vomits in stressful situations...........................0	1	2	3
Has panic attacks and seems overwhelmed by anxiety 0	1	2	3
Complains of racing heart rate 0	1	2	3
Has a tantrum or clings to adults when anxious 0	1	2	3
'Freezes' and can hardly move or speak when anxious 0	1	2	3

Anxious about being separated from parent

Fights or panics when being separated from parent.....................0	1	2	3
Worries about parents being OK when separated from them 0	1	2	3
Wants parent to stay while they fall asleep 0	1	2	3
Unwilling to sleep in own bedroom 0	1	2	3
Unwilling to sleep over at another person's house......................0	1	2	3
Worries about when parent is returning to pick them up...............0	1	2	3
Panics if parent is late to pick them up.....................................0	1	2	3

Specific phobias

Frightened of animals even though they are harmless.................................0   1   2   3

Frightened by clowns or other 'entertaining' characters............................0   1   2   3

Frightened of medical procedures, refuses treatment, panics.....................0   1   2   3

Very worried about everyday events such as storms or power cuts..............0   1   2   3

Panics in enclosed or crowded spaces 0   1   2   3

Unrealistically worried about germs, accidents or illness...........................0   1   2   3

Obsessions or compulsions

Obsessional behaviour, such as washing hands, counting steps 0   1   2   3

Has thoughts, images, or impulses that will not go away 0   1   2   3

Likes to follow an exact routine when eating or dressing............................0   1   2   3

Unusually upset by tragic events

Gets very upset by news about disasters, accidents, etc. 0   1   2   3

Plans elaborate escapes to avoid possible disasters..................................0   1   2   3

Worries about unlikely catastrophes...0   1   2   3

Needs excessive reassurance that they and their family are safe 0   1   2   3

Has an extreme reaction to a trauma they have experienced......................0   1   2   3

Social anxiety

Unreasonably shy with unfamiliar people 0   1   2   3

Unwilling to join in with other children..0   1   2   3

Over-sensitive and self-conscious, very easily embarrassed 0   1   2   3

Hates being watched 0   1   2   3

Very shy and reluctant to perform, even in a group 0   1   2   3

Positive characteristics and strengths (describe at least 3)

Important notes

This checklist can be used to help diagnose and assess Anxiety Disorder. However, several conditions have similar characteristics and there may a range of explanations for the observations made. Specialist assessment is necessary for a formal diagnosis.

- Supporting notes on Anxiety Disorder (pages 116–21)
- Guides for discussions with colleagues, parents and students (pages 184–8)

SUPPORTING NOTES ON ANXIETY DISORDER
Characteristics of Anxiety Disorder

A certain level of anxiety is a normal and healthy reaction to adverse or threatening events. Anxiety is part of the way in which adults and children protect themselves from harm by becoming alert to dangers and taking appropriate action. Natural caution about unfamiliar situations allows us to judge a situation before we let down our guard, sensible awareness of risks helps us to calculate what is safe, and looking ahead helps us to cope successfully with future events.

However, frequent, excessive or unrealistic anxiety can impair normal day-to-day living and seriously incapacitate the child, adolescent or adult. If this occurs the anxiety is classified as a clinical disorder.

Various levels and types of anxiety are appropriate at different developmental stages; for example, it is normal for a small child to show some level of separation anxiety when their parent leaves them for a short while but abnormal for a teenager to react in the same way. It is reasonable for a 16-year-old to be slightly anxious about their career choice; it is unreasonable for a 6-year-old to be worried about their future employment.

Anxiety Disorder can take various forms including generalized anxiety, social anxiety, separation anxiety, specific phobias, panic disorders, and Obsessive-Compulsive disorders.

All anxiety conditions are marked by feelings of fearfulness, worry and apprehension, which are often expressed both verbally and through behaviour. In generalized anxiety the apprehension may be 'free floating' and not tied to any particular situation. The child or adolescent may be preoccupied by a range of worries and be unable to put anxieties to one side. For example a child may sit in class deep in thought about 'What if . . . I got germs . . . what if Mum's headache is cancer . . . what if I get on the wrong bus . . . what if I get in trouble', and so on, endlessly thinking about alarming possibilities.

Anxiety can also lead to avoidance behaviours. A child anxious about making mistakes may hold back from attempting class work and resist trying anything new; a socially anxious adolescent may be so overwhelmed with worries about what to say and do in social situations that they stay at home rather than go out with friends.

Anxiety can also cause general agitation and restlessness, or nervous mannerisms may appear. Medical examination may show physical signs of anxiety such as an irregular pulse rate, increased sweating, stomach pains, disturbed sleep or muscle tension. Anxiety can make ADHD symptoms more extreme.

When under pressure some anxious children and adolescents may become obviously distressed, perhaps trying to escape by running away or hiding. Others may 'freeze' and become very withdrawn, whilst others may become defensive, angry and oppositional.

Causes of Anxiety Disorder

There is a distinct genetic component in Anxiety Disorders. Of course, there are temperamental differences between us all; partly inherited and partly due to our life experiences.

Stress factors such as learning difficulties, inappropriate parenting styles, social difficulties, family dysfunction, parental mental health problems or physical illness may well exacerbate an inherent tendency to be anxious. For example, we know that children with learning difficulties are, on the whole, more anxious than those without.

Anxiety can be exacerbated by inappropriate treatment by adults. Harsh treatment of fearful behaviour can increase anxiety levels by creating two sources of anxiety, the fear itself and the fear of the adult's harsh reaction.

On the other hand, adult collusion with the child's fears can also impede the development of the child's autonomy and coping mechanisms. For an example an over-protective parent can inadvertently increase their child's fears by giving excessive reassurance, which implies that something dreadful is about to occur. An anxious parent may inadvertently transmit their own anxieties and create increased anxiety in their child.

Conditions which may be mistaken for Anxiety Disorder

Autism Spectrum Disorder (Autism and Asperger Syndrome)

Students with an Autism Spectrum Disorder are often anxious, obsessional and inflexible, becoming agitated and distressed if things do not follow the expected pattern.

Child abuse

Children or adolescents who have been abused may appear to be overly anxious if the abuse is not known to adults making the judgment. Once the situation is known, the student's anxiety may be seen to be quite valid. Realistic and justified fears rule out a primary diagnosis of Anxiety Disorder.

Conditions which may occur alongside Anxiety Disorder

Autism Spectrum Disorder (Autism and Asperger Syndrome)

There is a recognized overlap between Autism Spectrum Disorder and Anxiety Disorder and both disorders can occur concurrently. Many children and adolescents with Autism Spectrum Disorder (Autism and Asperger Syndrome) have a marked Anxiety Disorder with regard to specific events or life in general.

Anxiety with Obsessive-Compulsive Disorder

Obsessive and compulsive behaviours are a symptom and a component of Anxiety Disorder.

Anxiety with Post Traumatic Stress Disorder (PTSD)

Children and adolescents diagnosed with PTSD generally have high levels of anxiety. Pre-existing anxiety will increase the risk of PTSD following a traumatic event.

Anxiety with Selective Mutism

Selective Mutism is a very specific form of Anxiety Disorder. There is a separate checklist for Selective Mutism on page 62.

Professionals supporting the student (Anxiety Disorder)

Teachers

Class teachers and student counsellors will in all probability work as a team with the student's parents to support the student with regard to their anxieties. This help will be generalized rather than specific therapy, aiming to build the child or adolescent's confidence through positive support and commonsense guidance.

Psychologists, psychiatrists and counsellors

A psychologist, student counsellor or psychiatrist may also be involved in helping to manage the Anxiety Disorder, most likely through a program of Cognitive Behavioural Therapy, possibly combined with medication, family therapy or other treatments as required.

Strategies for meeting the student's needs (Anxiety Disorder)

- Anxiety Disorder may require the expertise of a specialist in the treatment of anxiety.
- The standard treatment procedure is Cognitive Behavioural Therapy.
- This means that the therapist working with the anxious student helps the student move away from an emotional response toward a response that involves cognition and logic. This helps the student make a realistic appraisal of the situation, which in turn helps constrain the emotional response.
- Medication may be indicated, if the anxiety is severe or prolonged. This is usually used in combination with other approaches such as Cognitive Behavioural Therapy and needs to be prescribed by a medically qualified practitioner.
- Anxious students are more comfortable where they are in a predictable, secure, and nurturing environment. However, over-protection is unnecessary and potentially increases rather than reduces anxiety.
- Parents and teachers can work effectively in helping the child or adolescent with Anxiety Disorder. Demonstrating a confident, relaxed approach to life and its ups and downs helps the anxious child to see that difficulties can usually be overcome. Using logic and common sense to reduce worries is a useful way to counteract high levels of anxiety.
- With regards to specific anxieties and fears the best approach is to gradually build the child or adolescent's resilience by introducing graduated challenges that they can cope with.
- Professional therapists may use special techniques such as visualization and relaxation training. The parent or classroom teacher can help by providing relaxed,

playful opportunities with adult support in situations where the child would otherwise be anxious.

- If a student has a panic attack, it is important for adults to remain calm, speak quietly, and ensure that the student feels secure. It is important to remember that the student's reactions at this stage are driven by emotion, not logic, and so uncomplicated reassurances usually work best.

Recommended further reading (Anxiety Disorder)

Anxiety in Children

Author: Ved Varma
Date of publication: 2016
Publisher: Routledge

Child Anxiety Theory and Treatment

Editors: Andy Field and Sam Cartwright-Hatton
Date of publication: 2008
Publisher: Routledge

Freeing Your Child from Anxiety: Powerful, Practical Solutions to Overcome Your Child's Fears, Worries, and Phobias

Author: Tamar Chansky
Date of publication: 2004
Publisher: Crown Publishing Group

Helping Your Anxious Child: A Step by Step Guide for Parents

Authors: Ronald Rapee and Ann Wignall
Date of Publication: 2013
Publisher: New Harbinger

My Anxious Mind: A Teen's Guide to Managing Anxiety and Panic

Authors: Michael Tomkins and Katherine Martinez
Date of publication: 2009
Publisher: Magination Press

The Anxiety Cure for Kids: A Guide for Parents

Authors: Elizabeth DuPont Spencer, Robert DuPont and Caroline DuPont
Date of publication: 2003
Publisher: John Wiley & Sons

The Anxiety Workbook for Teens: Activities to Help You Deal with Anxiety and Worry

Author: Lisa Schab
Date of publication: 2008
Publisher: New Harbinger Publication

The Shyness and Social Anxiety Workbook for Teens: CBT and ACT Skills to Help You Build Social Confidence

Author: Jennifer Shannon
Date of publication: 2012
Publisher: New Harbinger Publications

Treating Childhood and Adolescent Anxiety: A Guide for Caregivers

Authors: Eli R. Lebowitz and Haim Omer
Date of Publication: 2013
Publisher: John Wiley & Sons

What to Do When You Worry Too Much: A Kid's Guide to Overcoming Anxiety

Author: Dawn Huebner
Date of publication: 2005
Publisher: Magination Press

Useful websites for Anxiety Disorder

www.nimh.nih.gov
National Institute of Mental Health. Research organization
Information for parents and teachers. USA

www.youngminds.org.uk
Young Minds. Not for Profit organization
Information for parents, teachers and young people. UK

www.nami.org
National Alliance on Mental Illness. Not for profit organization
Information for parents and teachers. USA

www.youthbeyondblue.org.au
Youth Beyond Blue. Not for Profit organization
Information for parents, teachers and young people. Australia

www.aacap.org
American Academy of Child and Adolescent Psychiatry. Professional organization
Information for parents and teachers. USA

References for Anxiety Disorder

American Psychiatric Association (2013) *Diagnostic and Statistical Manual of Mental Disorders, 5th Edition*, Washington, DC: APA.

Beidel, D.C. and Turner, S.M. (2005) *Childhood Anxiety Disorders: A Guide Research and Treatment*, London: Routledge.

Cobham, V. et al. (2017) 'Working with parents to treat anxiety disordered children', *Behaviour Research and Therapy*, 95, pp. 128–138.

Compton, S.N. et al. (2004) 'Cognitive-Behavioral psychotherapy for anxiety and depressive disorders in children and adolescents: an evidence-based review', *Journal of the American Academy of Child & Adolescent Psychiatry*, 43(8), pp. 930–959.

Degnan, K.A., Almas, A.N. and Fox, N.A. (2010) 'Temperament and the environment in the etiology of childhood anxiety', *Journal of Child Psychology and Psychiatry*, 51, pp. 497–517.

Fong, G. and Garralda, E. (2005) 'Anxiety disorders in children and adolescents', *Psychiatry*, 4(8), pp. 77–81.

Ginsburg, G.S., Riddle, M. and Davies, M. (2006) 'Somatic symptoms in children and adolescents with Anxiety Disorders', *Journal of the American Academy of Child & Adolescent Psychiatry*, 45(10), pp. 1179–1187.

Glatt, S.J., Faraone, S.V. and Tsuang, M.T. (2008) 'Mental health etiology: biological and genetic determinants', in Friedman, H. (Ed.), *International Encyclopedia of Public Health*, Oxford, UK: Academic Press, pp. 343–350.

Herzig-Anderson, K. et al. (2012) 'School-based anxiety treatments for children and adolescents', *Child and Adolescent Psychiatric Clinics of North America*, 21(3), pp. 655–668.

Morris, T.L. and March, J.S. (2004) *Anxiety Disorders in Children and Adolescents, 2nd Edition*, New York: Guilford Press.

Ost, L.-G. (2017) 'Brief, intensive and concentrated cognitive behavioural treatments for anxiety disorders in children: a systematic review and meta-analysis', *Behaviour Research and Therapy*, 97, pp. 134–145.

Rapee, R.M. (2012) 'Anxiety disorders in children and adolescents: nature, development, treatment and prevention', in Rey, J.M. (Ed.), *Textbook of Child and Adolescent Mental Health*, Geneva: International Association for Child and Adolescent Psychiatry and Allied Professions.

Scarpa, A. and Wilson, L. (2012)' Childhood Mental Disorders'. in Ramachandran, V.S. (Ed.), *Encyclopedia of Human Behavior, 2nd Edition*, London: Academic Press, pp. 467–475.

Sorenson, L. et al. (2011) 'Is behavioural regulation in children with ADHD aggravated by Comorbid Anxiety Disorder?' *Journal of Attention Disorders*, 15(1), pp. 56–66.

Strang, J.F. et al. (2012) 'Depression and anxiety symptoms in children and adolescents with autism spectrum disorders without intellectual disability', *Research in Autism Spectrum Disorders*, 6(1), pp. 406–412.

World Health Organization (2007) *ICIDH-2: International Classification of Functioning, Disability and Health – Children and Youth*, Geneva: WHO.

World Health Organization (2013) *International Classification of Diseases, 10th Edition, Clinical Modification*, Geneva: WHO.

DEPRESSION CHECKLIST

Glynis Hannell BA (Hons) MSc Psychologist

Name of child or adolescent   Age

Each item should be checked off using the following rating scale

0   Not at all, never occurs, does not apply
1   Mild, sometimes observed, applies to some extent
2   Moderate, often observed, certainly applies
3   Severe, frequently observed, strongly applies

Negative mood

Negative about most things	0	1	2	3
Complains of being 'fed up' or bored	0	1	2	3
Seems sad, cries easily	0	1	2	3
Seems flat and emotionless	0	1	2	3
Irritable and touchy	0	1	2	3
Disregards own safety and wellbeing	0	1	2	3

Loss of interest and enjoyment

Has lost interest in things that used to be enjoyed	0	1	2	3
Not interested if suitable activities are suggested	0	1	2	3
Limited sense of humour	0	1	2	3
Seems lazy and disinterested in most things	0	1	2	3
Does not seem to care about success in schoolwork or sports	0	1	2	3
Hard to please	0	1	2	3
Complains and finds fault	0	1	2	3

Social isolation

Sullen and uncommunicative	0	1	2	3
Will not willingly join in family or peer group activities	0	1	2	3
Stays alone in their room for long periods of time	0	1	2	3
Does not contact friends outside of school	0	1	2	3
Thinks people are deliberately trying to upset or annoy them	0	1	2	3
Reluctant to attend school	0	1	2	3

Peer group dependence

Engages in risky exploits with peers	0	1	2	3
Has excessive need to be with friends	0	1	2	3

Disturbed eating or sleeping patterns

	0	1	2	3
Has difficulty in getting to sleep or staying asleep	0	1	2	3
Sleeps an excessive amount or at unusual times	0	1	2	3
Eats much less than usual, not interested in food	0	1	2	3
Eats an excessive amount but may not be selective	0	1	2	3

Poor concentration

	0	1	2	3
Seems indecisive	0	1	2	3
Seems forgetful and poorly organized	0	1	2	3
Seems vague and inattentive	0	1	2	3

Low self-esteem

	0	1	2	3
Says they are stupid, dumb, etc.	0	1	2	3
Finds it hard to accept criticism	0	1	2	3
Finds it hard to accept praise or affection	0	1	2	3
Says they would be better off dead	0	1	2	3
Says parents prefer or favour other children in family	0	1	2	3
Says teachers prefer or favour others in class	0	1	2	3

Preoccupation with negative, violent, or morbid ideas

	0	1	2	3
Draws and writes on negative, violent, or morbid topics	0	1	2	3
Talks about suicide	0	1	2	3
Seems overly interested in violence and death	0	1	2	3
Takes risks that could be suicidal	0	1	2	3

Positive characteristics and strengths (describe at least 3)

Important notes

This checklist can be used to help diagnose and assess Depression. However, several conditions have similar characteristics and there may a range of explanations for the observations made. Specialist assessment is necessary for a formal diagnosis.

- Supporting notes on Depression (pages 124–9)
- Guides for discussions with colleagues, parents and students (pages 184–8)

SUPPORTING NOTES ON DEPRESSION

Characteristics of Depression

Children and adolescents who are depressed can seem sad, withdrawn and clearly depressed. They may resist inquiries about how they feel and say that there is nothing wrong, or they may complain of negative feelings such as boredom or loneliness rather than Depression.

Children and adolescents with Depression are often withdrawn and tend to isolate themselves, especially from close interpersonal contact. However, Depression can also lead to irritable, disruptive, angry, inattentive and very agitated behaviour.

Loss of energy, poor concentration and low motivation are strongly characteristic of Depression. This can easily be misread as laziness, disinterest or noncompliance. Sometimes a facade of exuberant, outgoing behaviour is used to disguise or deny feelings of Depression.

Depression often results in disturbed sleep, the child or adolescent usually finding it difficult to sleep or occasionally sleeping too much. Loss of appetite or indiscriminate comfort eating can also be a warning sign of Depression.

Negative thinking and thoughts of self-harm are often associated with Depression. In adolescents this may be disguised as risk-taking behaviour such as reckless driving or use of drugs or alcohol. Sometimes excessive concerns about physical health, with aches and pains that do not prove to have any organic origin, can be symptomatic of Depression.

Causes of childhood and adolescent Depression

The causes of Depression are complex and not necessarily well understood.

Depression can occur without any environmental triggers. It is known that irregularities in the chemicals in the brain, which are called neurotransmitters, and other changes in brain structure and chemistry are implicated in Depression. Depression may be genetic, so that the child or adolescent may have an inherited predisposition to Depression. Environmental events may, or may not, trigger this vulnerability.

There is research evidence that adverse events in early life can impact on brain development which in turn can increase the risk of Depression in childhood, adolescence or adulthood.

Negative social experiences (such as being bullied) or poor self-image (for example due to obesity) can lead to Depression.

Children and adolescents do of course sometimes experience very sad or traumatic events as part of normal living. There will be a natural period of grief or distress. Depression is diagnosed when the sad or negative feelings continue beyond the expected recovery time after such an event.

Conditions which may be mistaken for Depression

Attention-Deficit Disorder (inattentive type)

Children and adolescents who have the inattentive form of Attention-Deficit Disorder may often seem low in motivation and energy and 'in a world of their own.'

ADHD

Children and adolescents with ADHD can also be irritable and have a low frustration tolerance.

Oppositional Defiant Disorder

Negative, depressed mood can be an intrinsic part of Oppositional Defiant Disorder. The two conditions can also occur in parallel.

Child maltreatment

Children who are being (or have been) maltreated may also appear to be depressed. They may indeed have this clinical condition as part of their ongoing reaction to an abusive situation.

Ill health

Children who have a medical condition (perhaps not diagnosed) can also appear to be depressed. For instance, a child who has a sleep disorder, severe anaemia, or some other debilitating medical condition will seem low in motivation and flat in mood and may well present in a depressed state.

Conditions which may occur alongside Depression

Depression with anxiety

Some children and adolescents who are depressed also have an Anxiety Disorder

Depression with Conduct Disorder

It is common for antisocial, angry and delinquent children and adolescents diagnosed with Conduct Disorder to also be diagnosed with Depression.

Professionals supporting the student

Teachers

The classroom teacher will of course be of primary importance in recognizing the child or adolescent with depressed mood. The teacher may need to be particularly vigilant with regard to deterioration of mood.

Psychologists, counsellors or psychiatrists

A psychologist, counsellor or psychiatrist is likely to be involved if Depression significantly impairs social, academic, or other important areas of functioning. Counselling and medication are likely treatment options. Medication must be prescribed by a qualified medical practitioner.

Strategies for meeting the student's needs (Depression)

Strategies for recognizing Depression

- Arrange for appropriate further professional advice with regard to any child or adolescent who appears to be depressed, withdrawn, talks of self-harm or who seems to be low in motivation, irritable or cranky.

- Be particularly aware of the content of artwork and written language. Sometimes the darkest thoughts are expressed through drawing or writing.

- Communicate promptly with parents if you have any concerns about a child or adolescent who seems to be depressed.

Supportive strategies (Depression)

- Negative or irritable mood may well impact socialization – a small group of supportive peers perhaps monitored by an adult may provide the most supportive environment.

- Ensure there are plenty of supportive, positive experiences during school hours. Allow leeway with regard to work completion and give encouragement and support.

- Recognize that Depression cannot be overcome by advice to 'cheer up'. Depression is characterized by intractable negative mood, which is often very difficult to lift voluntarily.

- Find time to make personal contact and make clear that you are supportive during the 'tough patch' which is being experienced.

- Encourage a positive mood by showing how to interpret situations positively and how to deal with negatives constructively. Cognitive Behavioural Therapy (CBT) is demonstrated to be an effective treatment.

- Recognize that Depression does not have a logical basis, so that having everything necessary to feel happy and confident has little impact on a depressed person's state of mind.

- Ensure that the classroom environment is as positive and supportive as possible and that the class members all give each other mutual support and avoid negatives.

- Address any issues that may be contributing to negative, depressed feelings. Depression increases vulnerability to harassment and victimization, so monitor this carefully.

- Use positive, uplifting and inspiring stories, art and music to help counteract depressed feelings.

Recommended further reading for Depression

Beyond the Blues: A Workbook to Help Teens Overcome Depression

Author: Lisa Schab
Date of publication: 2008
Publisher: Instant Help Books

Coping with Depression in Young People: A Guide for Parents

Authors: Carol Fitzpatrick and John Sharry
Date of publication: 2004
Publisher: John Wiley & Sons

Depression and Your Child: A Guide for Parents and Caregivers

Author: Deborah Serani
Date of publication: 2013
Publisher: Rowman & Littlefield

Depression in Children and Adolescents

Authors: John Smith and Emily Klass
Date of publication: 2016
Publisher: Routledge

Depression: Cognitive Behaviour Therapy with Children and Young People (CBT with Children, Adolescents and Families)

Authors: Chrissie Verduyn, Julie Rogers and Alison Wood
Date of publication: 2009
Publisher: Routledge

Freeing Your Child from Negative Thinking: Powerful, Practical Strategies to Build a Lifetime of Resilience, Flexibility, and Happiness

Author: Tamar Chansky, PhD
Date of publication: 2008
Publisher: De Capo Press

Rescuing Your Teenager from Depression

Author: Norman Berlinger
Date of publication: 2005
Publisher: HarperCollins Publishers Inc

When Nothing Matters Anymore: A Survival Guide for Depressed Teens

Author: Bev Cobain
Date of publication: 2007
Publisher: Free Spirit Publishing

Useful websites for Depression

www.nimh.nih.gov
National Institute of Mental Health. Research organization
Information for parents and teachers. USA

www.youngminds.org.uk
Young Minds. Not for Profit organization
Information for parents, teachers and young people. UK

www.nami.org
National Alliance on Mental Illness. Not for profit organization
Information for parents and teachers. USA

www.healthyplace.com
Healthy Place. Media organization
Information for parents. USA

www.youthbeyondblue.org.au
Youth Beyond Blue. Not for profit organization
Information for parents, teachers and young people. Australia

www.aacap.org
American Academy of Child and Adolescent Psychiatry. Professional organization
Information for parents and teachers. USA

References for Depression

American Psychiatric Association (2013) *Diagnostic and Statistical Manual of Mental Disorders, 5th Edition*, Washington, DC: APA.

Bernaras, E. et al. (2011) 'Child Depression in the school context', *Procedia – Social and Behavioural Sciences*, 29, pp. 198–207.

Cairns, K. et al. (2015) 'Identifying prevention strategies for adolescents to reduce their risk of Depression. A Delphi consensus study', *Journal of Affective Disorders* 183, pp. 229–238.

Christ, S. et al. (2017) 'The joint impact of parental psychological neglect and peer isolation on adolescents' depression', *Child Abuse and Neglect*, 69, pp. 151–162.

D'Souza, S. et al. (2016) 'Environmental and genetic determinant of childhood Depression: the roles of *DAT 1* and the antenatal environment', *Journal of Affective Disorders*, 197, pp. 151–158.

Dubicka, B. (2012) 'Depression in adolescent girls: science and prevention', in Strauman, T.J., Costanzo, P.R. and J. Garber, J. (Eds.), *Child and Adolescent Mental Health*, London: Guilford Press.

Fergusson, E. (2007) 'If your adolescent has Depression or bipolar disorder', *Child and Adolescent Mental Health*, 12(2), https://doi.org/10.1111/j.1475-3588.2007.00450_8.x.

Gallerani, C.M., Garber, J. and Martin, N.C. (2010) 'The temporal relation between Depression and comorbid psychopathology in adolescents at varied risk for Depression', *Journal of Child Psychology and Psychiatry*, 51(3), pp. 242–249.

Gledhill, J. and Hodes, M. (2008) 'Depression and suicidal behaviour in children and adolescents', *Psychiatry*, 7(8), pp. 335–339.

Harrington, R. (2005) 'Depression and suicidal behaviour in children', *Psychiatry*, 4(8), pp. 85–88.

Hiroto, T. et al. (2016) 'Depression in children and adolescents', in Frodl, T. (Ed.), *Systems Neuroscience in Depression*, Oxford, UK: Academic Press, pp. 309–324.

Hollander, D. (2006) 'Symptoms of Depression in middle school teenagers linked to risky behaviour', *Perspectives on Sexual and Reproductive Health*, 38(4), pp. 230–234.

Inferna, M.R. et al. (2016) 'Associations between Depression and specific childhood experiences of abuse and neglect', *Journal of Affective Disorders* 190, pp. 47–55.

Lewis, K.K. et al. (2012) 'Do parents know best? Parent-reported vs child-reported Depression symptoms as predictors of future child mood disorder in a high-risk sample', *Journal of Affective Disorders*, 141(2), pp. 233–236.

Malouf, A.V. and Brent, D.A. (2012) 'Child and adolescent Depression overview: what works, for whom and how well?' *Child and Adolescent Psychiatric Clinics of North America*, 21(2), pp. 299–312.

Mendes, A.V. et al. (2012) 'Mothers with Depression, School-age children with Depression? A systematic review', *Perspectives in Psychiatric Care*, 48(33), pp. 138–148.

Paul, E. and Eckenrode, J. (2015) 'Childhood psychological maltreatment subtypes and adolescent depressive symptoms', *Child Abuse and Neglect*, 47, pp. 38–47.

Spirito, A. et al. (2011) 'Cognitive Behavioural Therapy for adolescent Depression and suicidality', *Child and Adolescent Psychiatric Clinics of North America*, 20(2), pp. 191–204.

Tompson, M. et al. (2017) 'A randomised clinical trial comparing family-focused treatment and individual supportive therapy for Depression in childhood and early adolescence', *Journal of the American Academy of Child and Adolescent Psychiatry*, 56(6), pp. 515–523.

Vitiello, B. (2009) 'Treatment of adolescent depression: what we have come to know', *Depression and Anxiety*, 26(5), pp. 393–395.

Weeks, D. et al. (2016) 'Developmental pathways linking childhood and adolescent internalising, externalising, academic competence and adolescent Depression', *Journal of Adolescence*, 51, pp. 30–40.

Wilson, C. (2010) 'Depression: Cognitive Behaviour Therapy with children and young people', *Child and Adolescent Mental Health*, 15(33), pp. 176–182.

World Health Organization (2007) *ICIDH-2: International Classification of Functioning, Disability and Health – Children and Youth*, Geneva: WHO.

OPPOSITIONAL DEFIANT DISORDER CHECKLIST

Glynis Hannell BA (Hons) MSc Psychologist

Name of child or adolescent   Age

Each item should be checked off using the following rating scale

0   Not at all, never occurs, does not apply
1   Mild, sometimes observed, applies to some extent
2   Moderate, often observed, certainly applies
3   Severe, frequently observed, strongly applies

Negative, unstable mood

Very irritable, frequently annoyed 0	1	2	3
Has an explosive temper..0	1	2	3
Over-reacts to situations 0	1	2	3
Unpredictable mood, swings from one extreme to the other 0	1	2	3
Takes a long time to get over an upset, hard to 'talk round' 0	1	2	3

Difficult to please

Does not seem to care about being praised or rewarded 0	1	2	3
Finds fault with gifts or treats that are given 0	1	2	3
Does not join in with things that others are enjoying...................0	1	2	3

Difficult to discipline

Refuses to comply with reasonable requests 0	1	2	3
Deliberately disobeys rules or finds loopholes in rules................0	1	2	3
Does not seem to care if punished 0	1	2	3
Becomes defiant when criticized or punished...............................0	1	2	3
Blames others for their own wrongdoing 0	1	2	3
Highly indignant about own innocence if blamed 0	1	2	3
Reluctant to apologize or make good a mistake 0	1	2	3
Justifies behaviour by saying rules or request were unreasonable................0	1	2	3

Lack of respect for adults

Uses body language and facial expression to defy adults............0	1	2	3
Threatens adults who attempt to impose discipline 0	1	2	3
Scoffs at what adults say or do...0	1	2	3
Talks about adults in a disrespectful way 0	1	2	3
Will not accept adult authority..0	1	2	3

Tries to make the adult look at fault	0	1	2	3
Very demanding of adults; expects them to accept orders	0	1	2	3

Deliberately annoys people

Does things which they know will annoy adults	0	1	2	3
Goes out of their way to upset or annoy siblings or peers	0	1	2	3
Won't stop annoying behaviour when asked to do so	0	1	2	3

Takes things very personally

Takes general criticism very personally	0	1	2	3
Cannot take constructive feedback, thinks it is criticism	0	1	2	3
Holds grudges for a long time	0	1	2	3

Undermines others' enjoyment

Will deliberately spoil others' fun	0	1	2	3
Ridicules success or popularity in others	0	1	2	3
Spoils surprises or secrets	0	1	2	3
Spiteful towards others	0	1	2	3

Associated problems

Has ADHD	0	1	2	3
Has learning difficulties	0	1	2	3
Has communication difficulties	0	1	2	3

Positive characteristics and strengths (describe at least 3)

Important notes

This checklist can be used to help diagnose and assess Oppositional Defiant Disorder. However, several conditions have similar characteristics and there may a range of explanations for the observations made. Specialist assessment is necessary for a formal diagnosis.

- Supporting notes on Oppositional Defiant Disorder (pages 132–7)
- Guides for discussions with colleagues, parents and students (pages 184–8)

SUPPORTING NOTES ON OPPOSITIONAL DEFIANT DISORDER

Characteristics of Oppositional Defiant Disorder

The child or adolescent who has Oppositional Defiant Disorder has marked difficulties in dealing with interpersonal interactions, particularly with adults.

One distinct characteristic of Oppositional Defiant Disorder is intense, rapid shifts of mood leading to the child or adolescent suddenly becoming very angry over minor provocations. Mood is often negative and irritable.

A child or adolescent with Oppositional Defiant Disorder may seem to deliberately provoke conflict by contradicting what is said, resisting reasonable requests, and ignoring established rules and conventions of behaviour. They may seem to go out of their way to challenge adults over both minor and major issues. Disrespect and rudeness are common elements of Oppositional Defiant Disorder

Some degree of oppositional defiant behaviour is normal at certain stages of development. In early childhood, there is a stage (usually between 2 and 3 years of age) in which children typically become noncompliant as they are beginning to learn to handle the complexities of interpersonal relationships and to manage the inevitable restrictions that are placed on them.

In adolescence some degree of oppositional behaviour may be seen as normal, and it is part of the process of the adolescent creating their own unique individuality.

Causes of Oppositional Defiant Disorder

The causes of Oppositional Defiant Disorder are complex, and each individual has their own set of causative factors. Traits such as irritability, impulsivity and a tendency to be headstrong may be innate and related to biological and/or genetic factors. Ineffective parenting styles are thought to contribute to the development of challenging and noncompliant behaviour, although a child with a difficult temperament may undermine what might otherwise be adequate parenting strategies.

There is increasing evidence of the close relationship between Oppositional Defiant Disorder and ADHD. Many ADHD children and adolescents show signs of Oppositional Defiant Disorder and vice versa, to the extent that some researchers suggest that Oppositional Defiant Disorder could be categorized as a sub set of ADHD.

Children or adolescents with Oppositional Defiant Disorder often use their noncompliant behaviour to disguise or compensate for feelings of personal inadequacy or their lack of alternative, socially acceptable ways of earning prestige and self-respect. Anxiety Disorder, Depression and Oppositional Defiant Disorder are very strongly linked.

Oppositional Defiant Disorder can be associated with family dysfunction, although it is very important to note that not all children experiencing the same family situation will develop oppositional defiant behaviours. There is a complex interplay of personality and situation.

Conditions which may be mistaken for Oppositional Defiant Disorder

Autism Spectrum Disorder

Children or adolescents with Autism Spectrum Disorder may show characteristics of Oppositional and Defiant Disorder.

Conduct Disorder

Conduct Disorder is a more extreme behaviour disorder than Oppositional Defiant Disorder and brings with it aggression toward people and animals, destruction of property, vandalism, theft, or dishonesty. Generally speaking, all of the features of Oppositional Defiant Disorder are included within Conduct Disorder, but Conduct Disorder is a more severe and widespread behavioural problem.

Intellectually gifted child or adolescent

Intellectually gifted children or adolescents placed in a situation in which their intellectual capacities are not recognized and channelled can sometimes appear to be oppositional and defiant in the way that they will challenge adults' opinions and decisions.

Intellectual Disability

Children and adolescents with an Intellectual Disability may become oppositional or defiant, particularly if their Intellectual Disability is not fully understood. Their difficulties with complying with reasonable requests and their limitations with interpersonal skills may be an intrinsic part of their Intellectual Disability.

Language Disorder

Some children or adolescents with language difficulties may also seem oppositional or defiant because they have problems in receptive language. This means that they do not fully understand what is said to them, and they may have difficulties formulating answers. If this is viewed as a behaviour problem, the child may become increasingly frustrated and behave inappropriately.

Conditions which may occur alongside Oppositional Defiant Disorder

Oppositional Defiant Disorder with Depression

Oppositional Defiant Disorder is marked by negative mood. Depression and Oppositional Defiant Disorder frequently co-exist.

Oppositional Defiant Disorder with ADHD

This is a very common combination. ADHD brings with it a tendency towards instability of mood, impulsiveness and high reactivity. These features are also common characteristics of Oppositional Defiant Disorder.

Professionals supporting the student (Oppositional Defiant Disorder)

Teachers

The class teacher will have a primary role, usually with the support of a specialist educator with expertise in behaviour management.

Counsellors, behaviour management specialists and social workers

School counsellors, behaviour management specialists and social workers may be involved to support classroom teachers and parents with regard to general management issues.

Psychologists and psychiatrists

A psychiatrist or psychologist is likely to have a significant role in diagnosis and in determining appropriate treatment and management strategies. This may include individual or group therapy for the child or adolescent, pharmaceutical therapy and family or parent support and training.

Strategies for meeting the student's needs (Oppositional Defiant Disorder)

- Arrange an appropriate assessment with a psychologist or psychiatrist with expertise in diagnosing behavioural disorders. It is important to eliminate the possibility that the child or adolescent has another underlying disorder such as Autism Spectrum Disorder or Intellectual Disability before treating the child or adolescent with a behavioural approach.

- Recognize that the child or adolescent with oppositional defiant behaviour may have concurrent issues with hyperactivity and impulsiveness. Depression and anxiety may also be relevant underlying factors. It is important to explore treatment options for the full range of presenting problems.

- Recognize that the child or adolescent with oppositional defiant behaviour may have a very limited repertoire of alternative thinking strategies and behaviours. Cognitive Behavioural Therapy is an appropriate approach to developing new, more appropriate and acceptable behaviours.

- Evaluate the trigger points for the child or adolescent's oppositional defiant behaviour, so that all parties understand what triggers the inappropriate behaviour and what types of management styles and environmental factors minimize the problems.

- Managing Oppositional Defiant Disorder is very much an exercise in networking and collaboration. It is important that all important adults in the child's or adolescent's life coordinate their efforts so that consistency is ensured.

- Appropriate parent training and support has been shown to have a positive impact and should be offered as part of the overall treatment approach.

- Preserving personal dignity is often very important for children or adolescents with Oppositional Defiant Disorder. Explore how the child or adolescent might be given ways to preserve their personal dignity in appropriate ways.

- Wherever possible, behavioural management needs to be dealt with in private so that the child or adolescent is not backed into a position in front of peers, where the only way to preserve their image is to continue to defy and oppose the adult. Children or adolescents who have cultivated an image as defiant and oppositional are very unlikely to agree to a 'deal' in front of their peers.

- Adults need to prioritize, so that the oppositional defiant child or adolescent has ample opportunity to feel that they are making their own decisions where this is appropriate.

- Issues that are matters of life or death, or that have serious safety or interpersonal risks need to be dealt with by the use of clear boundaries and explicit consequences. Make sure that the child or adolescent knows that these issues are not negotiable and that adults will do whatever is necessary to ensure that these rules are complied with.

- Invest time in building compliance and cooperation. Be there to follow through quickly. Refuse to engage in endless arguments but use your energy to devise alternatives that offer the child or adolescent acceptable (often face-saving) options and to follow through where necessary.

- It is very important that appropriate behaviour is teamed with a positive consequence to counterbalance the fact that inappropriate choices are followed through with negative consequences. However, this needs to be carefully handled, as children or adolescents with oppositional defiant behaviour tend to resist showing pleasure in treats or distress at punishments, so conventional rewards do not always work. Rewards that give some degree of responsibility and autonomy to the child or adolescent are often effective.

- Never promise positive consequences or threaten negative ones that you cannot deliver immediately after the child or adolescent has made a choice. Always follow through.

Recommended further reading for Oppositional Defiant Disorder

Challenging Behaviour in Young Children: Understanding, Preventing and Responding Effectively, 3rd Edition

Authors: Barbara Kaiser and Judy Sklar Rasminsky
Date of publication: 2011
Publisher: Pearson

Conduct and Oppositional Defiant Disorder

Editor: Cecilia Essau
Date of publication: 2003
Publisher: Routledge

10 Days to a Less Defiant Child: The Breakthrough Program for Overcoming Your Child's Difficult Behavior

Author: Jeffrey Berstein
Date of publication: 2006
Publisher: Da Capo Press

The Explosive Child: A New Approach for Understanding and Parenting Easily Frustrated and Chronically Inflexible Children

Author: Ross Greene
Date of publication: 2010
Publisher: HarperCollins

How to Reach and Teach Children with Challenging Behaviour (K-8); Practical Ready to Use Interventions That Work

Authors: Kaye Otten and Jodie Tuttle
Date of publication: 2010
Publisher: Jossey-Bass

Oppositional Defiant Disorder and Conduct Disorder, 2nd Edition

Author: Walter Matthys
Date of publication: 2017
Publisher: Wiley Blackwell

Parenting Tough Kids: Simple, Proven Strategies to Help Kids Succeed

Author: Mark Le Messurier
Date of publication: 2007
Publisher: Peytral Publications Inc

School Success for Kids with Emotional and Behavioral Disorders

Authors: Michelle Davis, Vincent Culotta, Eric Levine and Elizabeth Hess Rice
Date of publication: 2011
Publisher: Prufrock Press

Teaching Tough Kids: Simple and Proven Strategies for Student Success

Author: Mark Le Messurier
Date of publication: 2009
Publisher: David Fulton

Overcoming Defiance, Tantrums, and Other Everyday Behavior Problems by Seeing the World Through Your Child's Eyes

Author: Claudia Gold
Date of publication: 2011
Publishers: Da Capo Press

Useful websites for Oppositional Defiant Disorder

www.aacap.org.
American Academy of Child and Adolescent Psychiatry: Professional Organization
Information for parents and teachers. USA

www.kidsmatter.edu.au
Kids Matter: Government Service.
Information for parents and teachers. Australia

References for Oppositional Defiant Disorder

American Psychiatric Association (2013) *Diagnostic and statistical manual of mental disorders, 5th Edition*, Washington, DC: APA.

Burke, J.D. (2012) 'An affective dimension within oppositional defiant disorder symptoms among boys: personality and psychopathology outcomes into early adulthood', *Journal of Child Psychology and Psychiatry*, 53, pp. 1176–1183.

Burke, J.D. and Loeber, R. (2010) 'Oppositional Defiant Disorder and the explanation of the comorbidity between behavioral disorders and Depression', *Clinical Psychology: Science and Practice*, 17, pp. 319–326.

Da Fonseca, D. et al. (2010) 'How to increase academic performance in children with oppositional defiant disorder? An implicit theory effect', *Journal of Behavior Therapy and Experimental Psychiatry*, 41(3), pp. 234–237.

De la Osa, N. et al. (2016) 'Cognitive and affective components of Theory of Mind in preschooler with oppositional defiance disorder', *Psychiatry Research*, 241, pp. 128–134.

Dickerson Mayes, S. et al. (2012) 'Explosive, oppositional and aggressive behavior in children with autism compared to other clinical disorders and typical children', *Research in Autism Spectrum Disorders*, 6(1), pp. 1–10.

Ezpeleta, L. et al. (2012) 'Dimensions of oppositional defiant disorder in 3-year-old preschoolers', *Journal of Child Psychology and Psychiatry*, 53, pp. 1128–1138.

Finger, E.C. et al. (2012) 'Impaired functional but preserved structural connectivity in limbic white matter tracts in youth with conduct disorder or oppositional defiant disorder plus psychopathic traits', *Psychiatry Research: Neuroimaging*, 202(3), pp. 239–244.

Ghanizadeh, A. (2011) 'Should ADHD broaden diagnostic classification to include oppositional defiant disorder?' *Journal of Paediatrics and Child Health*, 47, pp. 396–397.

Greene, R.W. et al. (2007) 'Treatment of Oppositional Defiant Disorder in children and adolescents', in Barrett, P.M. and Ollendick, T.H. (Eds), *Handbook of Interventions that Work with Children and Adolescents: Prevention and Treatment*, Chichester, UK: John Wiley.

Handwerk, M. et al. (2012) 'Conduct, oppositional defiant, and disruptive behavior disorders', in Sturmer, P.M. and Hersen, M. (Eds), *Handbook of Evidence-Based Practice in Clinical Psychology*, Hoboken, NJ: John Wiley & Sons.

Nock, M.K. et al. (2007), 'Lifetime prevalence, correlates, and persistence of oppositional defiant disorder: results from the National Comorbidity Survey replication', *Journal of Child Psychology and Psychiatry*, 48, pp. 703–713.

Poulton, A.S. (2011) 'Time to redefine the diagnosis of oppositional defiant disorder', *Journal of Paediatrics and Child Health*, 47(6), pp. 332–334.

Prinz, R.J. and Dumas, J.E. (2007) 'Prevention of Oppositional Defiant Disorder and Conduct Disorder in children and adolescents', in Barrett, P.M. and Ollendick, T.H. (Eds), *Handbook of Interventions that Work with Children and Adolescents: Prevention and Treatment*, Chichester, UK: John Wiley & Sons.

Rhodes, S.M. et al. (2012) 'A comprehensive investigation of memory impairment in attention deficit hyperactivity disorder and oppositional defiant disorder', *Journal of Child Psychology and Psychiatry*, 53, pp. 128–137.

Siri, D. et al. (2017) 'Structural brain abnormalities of Attention Deficit/Hyperactivity Disorder with Oppositional Defiant Disorder', *Biological Psychiatry*, 82(9), pp. 642–650.

World Health Organization (2007) *ICIDH-2: International Classification of Functioning, Disability and Health – Children and Youth*, Geneva: WHO.

World Health Organization (2013) *International Classification of Diseases, 10th Edition, Clinical Modification*, Geneva: WHO.

CONDUCT DISORDER CHECKLIST

Glynis Hannell BA (Hons) MSc Psychologist

Name of child or adolescent   Age

Each item should be checked off using the following rating scale

0   Not at all, never occurs, does not apply
1   Mild, sometimes observed, applies to some extent
2   Moderate, often observed, certainly applies
3   Severe, frequently observed, strongly applies

Callous and uncaring

Appears to have little empathy or care for others.....................................0	1	2	3
Intolerant of the disadvantaged or disabled 0	1	2	3
Uncaring or cruel towards people and/or animals.......................................0	1	2	3
Enjoys cruel, sadistic, or violent films or games 0	1	2	3
Shows little guilt or remorse for wrongdoing..0	1	2	3

Destructive

Deliberately spoils or destroys other people's possessions 0	1	2	3
Vandalizes public property (graffiti, smashing glass, arson).........................0	1	2	3

Disrespectful of adult authority

Disobeys parents..0	1	2	3
Breaks school rules 0	1	2	3
Breaks the law 0	1	2	3
Runs away from home...0	1	2	3
Truants from school 0	1	2	3
Does not comply with punishments..0	1	2	3
Suspended or expelled from school..0	1	2	3
Defies authority figures 0	1	2	3
Does not respect other's rights..0	1	2	3

Physically or verbally aggressive

Starts fights or arguments...0	1	2	3
Uses physical force or a weapon to intimidate victim 0	1	2	3
Bullies or intimidates others...0	1	2	3
Talks aggressively or threatens violence 0	1	2	3

Deceitful and dishonest

Lies to adults 0   1   2   3
Lies to peers 0   1   2   3
Invents or exaggerates stories about self or others 0   1   2   3
Breaks promises 0   1   2   3
Cheats to get out of trouble...0   1   2   3
Blames others and does not accept responsibility.....................0   1   2   3

Illegal or anti-social behaviour

Uses illegal drugs 0   1   2   3
Deals in illegal drugs...0   1   2   3
Drinks alcohol or smokes cigarettes while underage..................0   1   2   3
Associates with other antisocial youngsters.............................0   1   2   3
Sexually promiscuous behaviour 0   1   2   3
Steals from family or friends..0   1   2   3
Steals from shops, school, or other organizations 0   1   2   3
Steals cars and drives them recklessly...................................0   1   2   3
Breaks into private premises and steals or vandalizes................0   1   2   3

Difficult at home

Often angry and uncooperative..0   1   2   3
Secretive and often absent from home 0   1   2   3
Aggressive towards weaker family members 0   1   2   3
Demanding and intimidating, must have needs met..................0   1   2   3
Does not communicate positively..0   1   2   3
Does not accept responsibility 0   1   2   3
Lacks warmth and empathy for family members........................0   1   2   3
Acts tough but is emotionally very immature 0   1   2   3

Positive characteristics and strengths (describe at least 3)

Important notes

This checklist can be used to help diagnose and assess Conduct Disorder. However, several conditions have similar characteristics and there may a range of explanations for the observations made. Specialist assessment is necessary for a formal diagnosis.

- Supporting notes on Conduct Disorder (pages 140–5)
- Guides for discussions with colleagues, parents and students (pages 184–8)

SUPPORTING NOTES ON CONDUCT DISORDER
Characteristics of Conduct Disorder

Conduct Disorder is marked by a major disturbance in the child or adolescent's social behaviour and in their relationship with others. A child or adolescent with Conduct Disorder will show frequent antisocial, disruptive, and delinquent behaviour, often leading to law breaking and sanctions from authority figures (suspension or expulsion from school or involvement with the juvenile justice system). The child or adolescent may damage property and exhibit aggression, violence, deceitfulness and other socially unacceptable behaviours.

The child or adolescent with Conduct Disorder will often have impaired empathy for other people and may particularly target weak or vulnerable adults or peers with intimidation, aggression, or other antisocial acts. Callous-unemotional traits are often associated with Conduct Disorder.

The child or adolescent with Conduct Disorder is much more likely than others to be involved with illegal drugs, weapons, or associated activities.

Causes of Conduct Disorder

Research evidence points to an underlying neurological basis for the disorder, frequently in association with high levels of impulsivity. Under-arousal (passive, 'switched off' behaviour) in the face of threats or punishments is also strongly related to Conduct Disorder.

Family dysfunction is also strongly implicated in Conduct Disorder. Parents may themselves have mental health or psychosocial difficulties, such as drug addiction. Lack of parental warmth, inconsistent discipline (including arbitrary and harsh punishments), parental aggression, child abuse and frequent changes of caregivers all appear to contribute to the emergence of Conduct Disorder. Failure at school and poor relationships with the mainstream peer group, combined with membership of an antisocial, delinquent peer group may maintain and increase inappropriate behaviour.

However, it is important to note that most children in an adverse environment do not develop Conduct Disorder, the conclusion being that an inter-play of neurobiological and environmental factors is a necessary condition for the development of Conduct Disorder.

Conditions which may be mistaken for Conduct Disorder
Oppositional Defiant Disorder

Oppositional Defiant Disorder shares some characteristics with Conduct Disorder in that both conditions involve noncompliance and oppositional behaviour. Conduct Disorder is a more severe behavioural disturbance and involves many more negative characteristics and behaviours than Oppositional Defiant Disorder alone.

Conditions which may occur alongside Conduct Disorder

Conduct Disorder with Depression

Negative mood is a strong component in Conduct Disorder and the two conditions often co-exist. However, the majority of children and adolescents with Depression do not develop Conduct Disorder.

Conduct Disorder with ADHD

These two conditions are often seen in tandem, and most child or adolescents with Conduct Disorder also have ADHD. It is important to note that the reverse is not true; the majority of child or adolescents with ADHD do not have Conduct Disorder.

Conduct Disorder with learning difficulties

Children or adolescents with Conduct Disorder are likely to have lower than average intelligence, poorer academic skills, and more specific difficulties with learning than their peers.

Professionals supporting the student

Teachers

The class teacher will have a primary role, usually with the support of a specialist educator with expertise in behaviour management.

Counsellors, behaviour management specialists and special educational facilities

The child or adolescent will almost certainly need specialist support from child or adolescent counsellors or behaviour management specialists. The child or adolescent may be placed in a special educational facility for behavioural management and support. In this case, specialist educators will certainly be involved.

Psychiatrists and psychologists

A psychiatrist or psychologist will also probably be involved in supporting the child or adolescent and those working with that child or adolescent at home and at school.

Social workers

A social worker may be involved in working with the child or adolescent and the family to address parenting and other issues.

Probation officers and youth workers attached to the justice system

A probation officer or other professional from a law enforcement agency may be involved because of the child or adolescent's antisocial and illegal behaviours.

Strategies for meeting the student's needs (Conduct Disorder)

- Recognize that Conduct Disorder may be due to an underlying neurobiological dysfunction.

- An inbuilt predisposition towards antisocial behaviour may be exacerbated by a dysfunctional family or community group. Abuse, neglect and inappropriate parenting may have played a significant role in the child or adolescent's development.

- Improved parenting skills will be likely to have a positive impact on both the parent's mental health and their child's behaviour. Appropriate professional intervention to develop improved parenting skills and support parental mental health will therefore be important.

- Provide appropriate social skills intervention for the child or adolescent to address issues such as poor social insight and inadequate interpersonal relationships.

- Many children and adolescents with Conduct Disorder are depressed, so ensure that this is considered and taken into account.

- Ensure that the teachers assigned to teach the child or adolescent are capable of maintaining the child or adolescent's compliance and cooperation in the classroom. Avoid placing the child or adolescent with teachers who do not have effective control of their classes, as the child or adolescent with Conduct Disorder is likely to become a major disruption.

- Anticipate that children or adolescents with Conduct Disorder are likely to have genuine learning difficulties along with their behavioural problems, and plan an appropriate program to suit the child or adolescents' learning needs.

- Give firm, consistent and fair behavioural boundaries and implement them quickly and confidently.

- Recognize and value the child or adolescent's positive qualities to help build his or her self-respect.

- Give opportunities for the child or adolescent to show empathy and compassion in a supported and supervised environment. For example, children or adolescents with Conduct Disorder may prove to be caring and responsible when caring for animals or younger children when with supportive adults and/or good role models.

- Make a particular effort to build up a positive relationship with the child or adolescent so that you can keep the channels of communication open.

- Ensure that consequences for unacceptable behaviour have a very direct and tangible link with what the child or adolescent has done. If the child or adolescent has defaced school property, then the appropriate punishment might be to restore the item to original condition or do enough hours of community service to earn enough to replace the damaged item. If the child or adolescent has intimidated or harassed another child or adolescent, then he or she should face that person to apologize and offer some form of recompense.

Recommended further reading for Conduct Disorder

Challenging Behaviour in Young Children: Understanding, Preventing and Responding Effectively, 3rd Edition

Authors: Barbara Kaiser and Judy Sklar Rasminsky
Date of publication: 2011
Publisher: Pearson

Cognitive-Behavioral Therapy for Anger and Aggression in Children

Authors: Denis G. Sukhodolsky PhD and Lawrence Scahill
Date of publication: 2012
Publisher: Guilford Press

10 Days to a Less Defiant Child: The Breakthrough Program for Overcoming Your Child's Difficult Behavior

Author: Jeffrey Berstein
Date of publication: 2006
Publisher: Da Capo Press

The Explosive Child: A New Approach for Understanding and Parenting Easily Frustrated and Chronically Inflexible Children

Author: Ross Greene
Date of publication: 2010
Publisher: HarperCollins

How to Reach and Teach Children with Challenging Behaviour (K-8): Practical Ready to Use Interventions That Work

Authors: Kaye Otten and Jodie Tuttle
Date of publication: 2010
Publisher: Jossey-Bass

Parenting Tough Kids: Simple, Proven Strategies to Help Kids Succeed

Author: Mark Le Messurier
Date of publication: 2007
Publisher: Peytral Publications Inc

Emotional and Behavioural Difficulties

Authors: Patrick McFarland, James Sanders and Bradley Hagan
Date of publication: 2016
Publisher: Routledge

School Success for Kids with Emotional and Behavioral Disorders

Authors: Michelle Davis, Vincent Culotta, Eric Levine and Elizabeth Hess Rice
Date of publication: 2011
Publisher: Prufrock Press

Taming Aggression in Your Child: How to Avoid Raising Bullies, Delinquents, or Trouble-Makers

Author: Parens Henri
Date of Publication: 2011
Publisher: Jason Aronson

Teaching Tough Kids: Simple, Proven Strategies for Student Success

Author: Mark Le Messurier
Date of publication: 2009
Publisher: David Fulton

Useful websites for Conduct Disorder

www.aacap.org.
American Academy of Child and Adolescent Psychiatry. Professional Organization Information for parents and teachers. USA

www.kidsmatter.edu.au
Kids Matter: Government Service.
Information for parents and teachers. Australia

References for Conduct Disorder

Aghajani, M. et al. (2017) 'Disorganised amygdala networks in conduct disordered juvenile offenders with callous-unemotional traits', *Biological Psychiatry*, 82(4), pp. 283–293.

American Psychiatric Association (2013) *Diagnostic and Statistical Manual of Mental Disorders, 5th Edition*, Washington, DC: APA.

Berkout, O.V., Young, J.N. and Gross, A.G. (2011) 'Mean girls and bad boys: recent research on gender differences in conduct disorder', *Aggression and Violent Behavior*, 16(6), pp. 503–511.

Bowden, J.M., Fergussen, D.M and Horwood, J. (2010) 'Risk factors for Conduct Disorder and Oppositional/Defiant Disorder: evidence from a New Zealand birth cohort', *Journal of American Academy of Child & Adolescent Psychiatry*, 49(11), pp. 1125–1133.

Cappadocia, M.C. et al. (2009) 'Contextualizing the neurobiology of conduct disorder in an emotion dysregulation framework', *Clinical Psychology Review*, 29(6), pp. 506–518.

Furlong, M. et al. (2012) 'Behavioural and cognitive-behavioural group-based parenting programmes for early-onset conduct problems in children aged 3 to 12 years', *Cochrane Database of Systematic Reviews*, 2012:2. Article number CD008225.

Hughes, T.L., Crothers, L.M. and Jimerson, S.R. (2010) *Identifying, Assessing, and Treating Conduct Disorder at School (Developmental Psychopathology at School)*, New York: Springer.

Liabo, K. and Richardson, J. (2007) *Conduct Disorder and Offending Behavior in Young People: Findings from Research (Child and Adolescent Mental Health)*, London: Jessica Kingsley.

Murrihy, R.C., Kidman, A.D. and Ollendick, T.H. (Eds) (2010) *Clinical Handbook of Assessing and Treating Conduct Problems in Youth*, New York: Springer.

Rubia, K. (2011) '"Cool" inferior frontostriatal dysfunction in Attention-Deficit/Hyperactivity Disorder versus "hot" ventromedial orbitofrontal-limbic dysfunction in Conduct Disorder: a review', *Biological Psychiatry*, 69(12), pp. 69–87.

Sasayama, D. et al. (2010) 'Neuroanatomical correlates of Attention-Deficit–Hyperactivity Disorder accounting for comorbid oppositional defiant disorder and Conduct Disorder', *Psychiatry and Clinical Neurosciences*, 64, pp. 394–402.

Smaragdi, A. (2017) 'Sex differences in the relationship between Conduct Disorder and cortical structure in adolescents', *Journal of the American Academy of Child & Adolescent Psychiatry*, 56(8), pp. 703–712.

Smith, C.S and Hung, L. (2012) 'The relative influence of conduct problems and Attention-Deficit Hyperactivity Disorder in the development of adolescent psychopathy', *Aggression and Violent Behavior*, 17(5), pp. 575–580.

Tackett, J.L. et al. (2011) 'Shared genetic influences on negative emotionality and major Depression/Conduct Disorder comorbidity', *Journal of American Academy of Child & Adolescent Psychiatry*, 50(8), pp. 818–827.

World Health Organization (2007) *ICIDH-2: International Classification of Functioning, Disability and Health – Children and Youth*, Geneva: WHO.

World Health Organization (2013) *International Classification of Diseases, 10th Edition, Clinical Modification*, Geneva: WHO.

MALTREATMENT, ABUSE AND BULLYING CHECKLIST

Glynis Hannell BA (Hons) MSc Psychologist

Name of child or adolescent   Age

Each item should be checked off using the following rating scale

0   Not at all, never occurs, does not apply
1   Mild, sometimes observed, applies to some extent
2   Moderate, often observed, certainly applies
3   Severe, frequently observed, strongly applies

Withdrawn behaviour

Seems remote and 'switched off'..0   1   2   3
Seems sullen and uncommunicative 0   1   2   3
Spends excessive time on computer games and/or social media.................0   1   2   3
Seems tired and unwilling to work or play 0   1   2   3
Does not want talk or write about himself or herself................................0   1   2   3
Refuses/anxious to go to school; does not want to leave parent.................0   1   2   3
Is secretive at home or at school 0   1   2   3
Often wants to go to the medical room or be taken home 0   1   2   3

Social difficulties

Overly possessive of one or two friends..0   1   2   3
Rejects friendship when it is offered...0   1   2   3
Seems isolated from peer group 0   1   2   3
Tries to buy friends 0   1   2   3
Erratic; is friendly one day, unfriendly the next 0   1   2   3
Bad tempered and easily annoyed...0   1   2   3
Verbally and physically aggressive 0   1   2   3

Explicit sexual behaviour

Engages in sexually explicit play...0   1   2   3
Makes sexually explicit comments or jokes...0   1   2   3
Draws attention to own body or private parts 0   1   2   3
Masturbates in sight of others..0   1   2   3
Overly interested in bodily functions such as urination 0   1   2   3
Tells untrue stories about sexual encounters with unlikely people 0   1   2   3
Makes sexually suggestive approaches to adults 0   1   2   3

Negative change in behaviour, attitude or school work

Schoolwork has deteriorated 0   1   2   3
Displays a more negative attitude toward learning...................................0   1   2   3
Is less easy going than previously..0   1   2   3
Takes less pride in self and achievements 0   1   2   3
Less well behaved than previously 0   1   2   3
Change in eating patterns (eats too much or too little)..............................0   1   2   3
Regression to thumb sucking, soiling, bed wetting, soft toy.......................0   1   2   3

Moody, emotional behaviour

Cries very readily, seems irritable and easily upset...................................0   1   2   3
Unnecessarily apologetic and ingratiating 0   1   2   3
Avoids eye contact, defensive body language...0   1   2   3
Very clingy to adult or special friend 0   1   2   3
Wants a lot of reassurance..0   1   2   3
Obsessional about cleanliness or neatness...0   1   2   3
Appears angry and defiant...0   1   2   3
Engages in very risky behaviour...0   1   2   3

Other disorders are apparent

Signs of low self-esteem (see Low self-esteem checklist) 0   1   2   3
Signs of Depression (see Depression checklist)...0   1   2   3
Signs of Conduct Disorder (see Conduct Disorder checklist).........................0   1   2   3

Signs of distress in artwork or writing

Depicts angry, violent or tragic themes in artwork......................................0   1   2   3
Produces very restrained, cautious, timid artwork.......................................0   1   2   3
Writes stories on angry, violent or tragic themes 0   1   2   3
Sexually explicit drawings or stories 0   1   2   3

Self-harm

Has self-inflicted injuries such as cuts, burns 0   1   2   3
Talks about or attempts suicide..0   1   2   3

Signs of physical harm by others

Unexplained bruises, burns, or other signs of injury.....................................0   1   2   3
Unwilling to undress for swimming, physical education and so on.................0   1   2   3
Frequently absent from school...0   1   2   3
Frequent complaints of not feeling well, visits sick room often 0   1   2   3

Positive characteristics and strengths (describe at least 3)

Important notes

This checklist can be used to help recognize if a student is being maltreated, abused or bullied. However, several conditions have similar characteristics and there may a range of explanations for the observations made. Specialist assessment is necessary for a formal diagnosis.

- Supporting notes on maltreatment, abuse and bullying (pages 148–53)
- Guides for discussions with colleagues, parents and students (pages 184–8)

SUPPORTING NOTES ON MALTREATMENT, ABUSE AND BULLYING

Overview of maltreatment, abuse and bullying

The terms 'maltreatment' and 'abuse' are sometimes used interchangeably; sometimes 'maltreatment' is used as an umbrella term for all types of inappropriate treatment and sometimes the term refers to acts of neglect and omission rather than deliberate abuse. Bullying generally refers to peer to peer behaviour but can also apply to adult to child interactions.

The World Health Organization states that:

> Child maltreatment is the abuse and neglect that occurs to children under 18 years of age. It includes all types of physical and/or emotional ill-treatment, sexual abuse, neglect, negligence and commercial or other exploitation, which results in actual or potential harm.

Being treated kindly, fairly and respectfully by others is an important foundation of every child's psychological and physical wellbeing. For the purposes of this checklist we look for behavioural signs that the child or adolescent is experiencing some form of physical, psychological or sexual abuse, neglect, bullying (including cyber bullying) or exploitation and is traumatized as a result.

Victims of any form of maltreatment may be very reluctant to speak out about what is happening to them or to seek support.

The reasons for this secrecy can be complex and difficult to counteract. The victim of abuse may feel that they are in some way to blame for what is happening to them and feel too ashamed to speak out. The abuser or bully may have intimidated the victim into silence or the victim may fear that they will not be believed. The victim may fear the consequences of speaking out, for example of getting a loved adult into trouble or triggering an increase, not decrease in harassment by peers.

Causes of maltreatment, abuse and bullying

Child maltreatment or abuse in any form is a complex social issue, and the pathology relates to the abusers rather than the children and adolescents who are their victims.

Social factors such as mental illness, drug or alcohol dependence or family and community dysfunction can increase the risk of an adult or peer maltreating a child or adolescent; however, favourable family and community circumstances do not necessarily prevent abuse from occurring.

Some children and adolescents are more vulnerable to maltreatment than others, because of intellectual and other forms of disability, because they are less socially or emotionally robust than their peers or because the abuser is an authority figure in the family, school or community.

Every jurisdiction has strict laws against child abuse in any form and in most countries professionals in contact with young people have a statutory duty to report suspected abuse to the relevant authorities.

Conditions which may be mistaken for the consequences of maltreatment, abuse and bullying

Depression

Depressed students often have behaviour patterns quite similar to those shown by maltreated, abused or bullied students, such as being withdrawn, negative, and uncommunicative.

Conditions which may occur alongside the consequences of maltreatment, abuse and bullying

Child maltreatment, abuse or bullying with Depression

Maltreatment, abuse or bullying can be the cause of Depression and this may continue for a long time after the abuse has stopped.

Child maltreatment, abuse or bullying with other disabilities or disorders

Naiveté and difficulties with social judgment are common in Intellectual Disability and Autism Spectrum Disorder, and this increases the risk of abuse and bullying. Other developmental disorders such as ADHD, chronic health conditions and physical disabilities can also increase vulnerability.

Professionals supporting the student (maltreatment, abuse and bullying)

Teachers

All developed countries have legislation to ensure that children and adolescents are protected from maltreatment and abuse. This generally means that professionals such as teachers have a mandatory duty to report cases of known or suspected child abuse to the appropriate authority.

Bullying is also subject to strong policy directives in schools and in some places will constitute indictable behaviour.

Child protection team

Usually there will be a child protection team (social worker, psychiatrist, psychologist, legal adviser) available to offer ongoing counselling and support. Family members may also be in need of counselling and support for themselves from the child protection team. Legal professionals will also be involved if the case becomes the subject of court action.

Alternative caregivers (foster parents)

Foster parents or other caregivers may become key adults if the abused child or adolescent is removed from an abusive home.

Strategies to meet the students' needs (maltreatment, abuse and bullying)

Strategies for recognizing and reporting

- Remember that you are almost certainly required by law to report suspected maltreatment or abuse to an authority that has responsibility for child protection, not just to your colleagues or school administration. Check the reporting procedure of your school or organization and the statutory authority and make sure that you have followed all the required steps.

- With regard to bullying, all professionals will be subject to policies and procedures that require them to act as soon as they become aware that a child or adolescent is being bullied.

- Document and date your concerns in detail and keep your records secure and confidential.

- If appropriate, discuss your concerns with the parents, but make it clear if you have a legal obligation to report to the appropriate authority.

Strategies for protecting against maltreatment, abuse and bullying

- Teach appropriate protective behaviours, including

  - discussing how to recognize potentially abusive situations

  - teaching that everyone has the right to feel safe and to be safe

  - teaching and practicing assertive, self-protective behaviours

  - discussing contingency plans for dealing with abuse or bullying

  - identifying a trusted adult to tell if abuse or bullying occurs

  - providing the telephone number of a reputable helpline

  - clearly stating that reports of abuse or bullying will be taken seriously

  - clearly stating that anyone reporting abuse or bullying will be given protection from the abuser

  - clearly stating that anyone reporting abuse or bullying will not be in trouble themselves

Strategies for dealing with the outcomes of maltreatment, abuse and bullying

- Ensure that the classroom environment is as supportive, consistent and nurturing as possible.
- Work as a team with other professionals and parents or caregivers to ensure that there is a network of support and a coordinated response.
- Monitor emotional and social wellbeing and continue to report matters of concern to the appropriate professionals.

Recommended further reading on maltreatment, abuse and bullying

The APSAC Handbook on Child Maltreatment

Authors: John E.B. Myers, APSAC (American Professional Society on the Abuse of Children)
Date of publication: 2010
Publisher: Sage Publications

Child Abuse: Today's Issues

Authors: Kimberly McCabe and Daniel Murphy
Date of publication: 2016
Publisher: Routledge

Child Abuse and Neglect, 2nd Edition

Authors: Monica McCoy and Stefanie Keen
Date of publication: 2013
Publisher: Routledge Academic

Child Maltreatment: Expanding Our Concept of Helping

Editors: Michael Rothery and Gary Cameron
Date of publication: 2016
Publisher: Routledge

School Bullying and Mental Health: Risks, Intervention and Prevention

Editors: Helen Cowie and Carrie-Anne Myers
Date of publication: 2017
Publisher: Routledge

Understanding Child Abuse and Neglect, 8th Edition

Author: Cynthia Crosson-Tower
Date of publication: 2009
Publisher: Pearson

Useful websites for maltreatment, abuse and bullying

www.nspcc.org.uk
National Society for the Prevention of Cruelty to Children. Not for profit organization
Information for parents and teachers. UK

www.youngminds.org.uk
Young Minds. Not for profit organization
Information for parents, teachers and young people. UK

www.childwelfare.gov
Child Welfare. Government organization
Information for parents and teachers. USA

www.childhelp.org
Child Help. Not for profit organization
Information for parents and teachers. USA

www.aacap.org
American Academy of Child and Adolescent Psychiatry Professional Organization
Information for parents and teachers. USA

www.childhood.org.au
Australian Childhood Foundation. Not for profit organization
Information for parents and teachers. Australia

References for maltreatment, abuse and bullying

Berlin, L.J., Appleyard, K. and Dodge, K.A. (2011) 'Intergenerational continuity in child maltreatment: mediating mechanisms and implications for prevention', *Child Development*, 82, pp. 162–176.

Boulton, M. et al. (2017) 'Perceived barriers that prevent high school students seeking help from teachers for bullying and their effects on disclosure intentions', *Journal of Adolescence*, 56, pp. 40–51.

Bruce, L.C. et al. (2012) 'Childhood maltreatment and social anxiety disorder: implications for symptom severity and response to pharmacotherapy', *Depression and Anxiety*, 29, pp. 132–139.

Debowska, A. et al. (2017) 'What do we know about child abuse and neglect patterns of co-occurance? A systematic review of profiling studies and recommendations for future research', *Child Abuse and Neglect*, 70, pp. 100–111.

Hanson, J. et al. (2017) 'Early adversity and learning: implications for typical and atypical behaviour', *Journal or Child Psychiatry and Psychology*, 58(7), pp. 770–778.

Jaffee, S.R. and Maikovich-Fong, A.K. (2011) 'Effects of chronic maltreatment and maltreatment timing on children's behavior and cognitive abilities', *Journal of Child Psychology and Psychiatry*, 52, pp. 184–194.

Ju, S. and Lee, Y. (2018) 'Developmental trajectories and longitudinal mediation effects of self-esteem, peer attachment, child maltreatment and depression on early adolescents', *Child Abuse and Neglect*, 76, pp. 353–363.

Kim, J. and Cicchetti, D. (2010) 'Longitudinal pathways linking child maltreatment, emotion regulation, peer relations, and psychopathology', *Journal of Child Psychology and Psychiatry*, 51, pp. 706–716.

McEachern, A.G., Aluede, O. and Kenny, M.C. (2008) 'Emotional abuse in the classroom: implications and interventions for counselors', *Journal of Counseling & Development*, 86, pp. 3–10.

Merritt, D. (2009) 'Child abuse potential: correlates with child maltreatment rates and structural measures of neighborhoods', *Children and Youth Services Review*, 31(8), pp. 927–934.

Penelope, K. et al. (2011) 'Variations in emotional abuse experiences among multiply maltreated young adolescents and relations with developmental outcomes', *Child Abuse & Neglect*, 35(10), pp. 876–886.

Schaeffer, P., Leventhal, J.M. and Gottsegen, A. (2011) 'Children's disclosures of sexual abuse: learning from direct inquiry', *Child Abuse & Neglect*, 35(5), pp. 343–352.

Shiakou, M. (2012) 'Representations of attachment patterns in the family drawings of maltreated and non-maltreated children', *Child Abuse Review*, 21, pp. 203–218.

Sidebotham, P. and Appleton, J.V. (2012) 'Understanding complex systems of abuse: institutional and ritual abuse', *Child Abuse Review*, 21, pp. 389–393.

Simmel, C. and Shpiegel, S. (2013) 'Describing the context and nature of emotional maltreatment reports in children', *Children and Youth Services Review*, 35(4), pp. 626–633.

Stalker, K. and McArthur, K. (2012) 'Child abuse, child protection and disabled children: a review of recent research', *Child Abuse Review*, 21, pp. 24–40.

Trickett, P. et al. (2011) 'Child maltreatment and adolescent development', *Journal of Research on Adolescence*, 21, pp. 3–20.

World Health Organization (2016) *Child Maltreatment Fact Sheet*, Geneva: WHO.

IMMATURITY CHECKLIST

Glynis Hannell BA (Hons) MSc Psychologist

Name of child or adolescent   Age

Each item should be checked off using the following rating scale

0   Not at all, never occurs, does not apply
1   Mild, sometimes observed, applies to some extent
2   Moderate, often observed, certainly applies
3   Severe, frequently observed, strongly applies

Play and recreation

Prefers to play with younger children	0	1	2	3
Prefers toys and activities usually enjoyed by younger children	0	1	2	3
Enjoys stories or TV programs suitable for younger children	0	1	2	3
Continues with imaginative, make-believe play longer than most	0	1	2	3
Frightened by films or stories usually enjoyed by their age group	0	1	2	3

Socially immature

Does not initiate friendships or play with own age group	0	1	2	3
Easily intimidated by children in own age group or older	0	1	2	3
Seeks adults to sort out small problems or upsets	0	1	2	3
Naïve and innocent for age, trusting, easily led	0	1	2	3
Uninhibited; says or does things that are inappropriate for age	0	1	2	3
Shy with strangers	0	1	2	3
Less aware of current affairs than others of same age	0	1	2	3
Less 'street smart' than most of own age group	0	1	2	3

Dependent

Worries about separating from parents	0	1	2	3
More dependent than most of their age group	0	1	2	3
Dependent on one or two special friends at school	0	1	2	3
Reluctant to be left with a babysitter	0	1	2	3
Reluctant to go to sleep overs or school camp	0	1	2	3
Reluctant to make simple decisions; wants adult to decide	0	1	2	3
Follows the group; is unwilling to stand up for themselves	0	1	2	3
Does not like to be given responsibility appropriate to age	0	1	2	3

Immature habits

Late to stop sucking thumb	0	1	2	3
Late to give up security blanket or soft toy	0	1	2	3

Concentration

Concentrates less well than most of own age group	0	1	2	3
More playful, less able to settle to work than others of same age	0	1	2	3

More physically restless in school than most of own age group 0	1	2	3
Less able to handle delays than most of own age group 0	1	2	3

Academically immature

Is not up to age standard with literacy...0	1	2	3
Is not up to age standard with mathematics 0	1	2	3
Needs more adult support with learning...0	1	2	3
Does not ask for help when it is needed..0	1	2	3
Immature handwriting, drawing or bookwork...0	1	2	3
Poor organization of schoolwork..0	1	2	3
Does not take the initiative in learning 0	1	2	3

Immature language

Immature speech...0	1	2	3
Limited general knowledge or vocabulary for their age 0	1	2	3
Later than average learning to talk 0	1	2	3

Physical immaturity

Less physical stamina than other children of the same age 0	1	2	3
Less well developed fine and/or gross motor skills 0	1	2	3
Physically smaller than most of own age group 0	1	2	3
Needs more sleep than most of own age group.......................................0	1	2	3
First teeth were later than usual 0	1	2	3
Late to reach puberty 0	1	2	3

Actual age compared with average age of peers

Child or adolescent's age is . . . years . . . months

Average age of peers is . . . years . . . months

Positive characteristics and strengths (describe at least 3)

Important notes

This checklist can be used to help diagnose and assess immaturity. However, several conditions have similar characteristics and there may a range of explanations for the observations made. Specialist assessment is necessary for a formal diagnosis.

- Supporting notes on immaturity (pages 156–9)
- Guides for discussions with colleagues, parents and students (pages 184–8)

SUPPORTING NOTES ON IMMATURITY

Characteristics of immaturity

Immaturity is not a disorder or disease, but it is often used to explain a child or adolescent's behaviour or learning style. Rates of physical, cognitive, emotional and social development do vary, and inevitably in any age group, some will be less mature than others. Under stress, such as the arrival of a new sibling, change of school or illness of a parent, temporary regression of maturity is quite normal.

Sometimes immaturity is only evident in social and emotional development, with other aspects of development progressing normally; in other cases, development seems to be delayed across all areas.

If immaturity is pervasive or extreme parents and teachers will want to investigate further. This is wise as global or extreme immaturity is usually a symptom of an underlying disorder, difficulty or disability. The checklist provided can help you to identify the pattern of any apparent immaturities. Sometimes this will lead to consideration of other diagnostic categories such as Anxiety Disorder or Intellectual Disability.

It should be noted that the terms 'developmental delay' or 'global developmental delay' are not synonymous with 'immaturity'. Developmental delay or global developmental delay are terms used to describe children who are too young to be formally diagnosed, but who in all probability have serious developmental impairments.

Causes of immaturity

There is no one cause of immaturity. There is natural variation in the emergence of language and problem solving, the development of resilience and independence and the unfolding of physical maturity.

Underlying minor, but chronic health problems such as recurring ear infections, sleep apnea, digestive disorders, anaemia and so on (which may or may not be diagnosed) can easily reduce resilience and increase dependency. This can in turn give the impression of general immaturity, so physical wellbeing should always be thoroughly checked.

While it is important to consider the intrinsic personality of the child, parenting style will also be a significant factor. Parents can shape their child's development. For example, one parent may build resilience by promoting their child's independence and allowing sensible levels of risk taking, whilst another may be more protective and hold back emerging maturity in the interests of keeping the child safe. Immature behaviour such as unnecessary crying can also be used by the child to manipulate adults if this proves to be effective.

Insecurity and social instability can also contribute to immaturity. The child who has had an unstable pattern of caregivers and family situations, or who has been psychologically or physically abused, is unlikely to mature in the same way as a child who has been in a secure, stable and loving environment.

Conditions which may be mistaken for immaturity

As indicated in the previous sections, it is often the case that what is described as immaturity is in fact a disorder or disability, often in a mild and not easily identified form. Immaturity or delay in a specific area of development can be intrinsic elements of the following categories of special need:

Intellectual Disability
Specific Learning Disorders
ADHD
Language Disorder
Anxiety Disorder
Selective Mutism
Developmental Coordination Disorder
Conduct Disorder
Oppositional Defiant Disorder
Child maltreatment or abuse
Asperger Syndrome

Professionals supporting the student (immaturity)

Teachers

Teachers will have the primary duty of care in school and may offer programs to develop increased maturity, in consultation with parents.

Family doctors and paediatricians

Family doctors or paediatricians can check physical health and development.

Psychologists

A psychologist with expertise in the diagnosis of childhood difficulties and disorders can provide a comprehensive assessment to ensure that the observed immaturities are not, in fact, symptomatic of an underlying disorder or disability.

Social workers, counsellors, psychiatrists and psychologists

A social worker, counsellor, or psychiatrist may be involved in supporting the family in the provision of developmentally appropriate opportunities to encourage the development of appropriate maturity.

Strategies for meeting the student's needs (immaturity)

Strategies for assessing immaturity

- Arrange for a medical check to rule out any underlying health problems.
- If immaturity is noted but not a major concern work with parents to devise strategies for meeting the student's needs, promoting increased independence and maturity.
- If immaturity is causing adults significant concern then arrange for a developmental assessment to identify any problems with intellectual, language, social or emotional development.

Strategies for managing social and emotional immaturity

- Encourage and support good parenting practices to encourage more autonomy and independence.

- Introduce graduated challenges to extend social and emotional resilience in small increments. Too big a leap in demands for maturity will be counterproductive.

- Use good role models and peer support to develop mature problem solving strategies when difficulties are encountered.

- Use discussion about characters in stories and films to model and teach mature behaviour and appropriate emotional responses.

- Encourage all adults to be confident and supportive when more mature behaviours or emotions are shown by the child or adolescent.

- Encourage all adults to accept that risks will be encountered and mistakes made as development proceeds as a normal part of growing up.

- Ensure that mature behaviour is encouraged and that immature behaviour does not reap rewards such as increased attention or adult indulgence.

- Arrange for the family to receive appropriate counselling if the parenting style or family circumstances seem to be contributing to social or emotional immaturity.

Strategies for pervasive immaturity (immaturity in several areas)

- Look at assessment results to see if the observed levels of maturity are consistent with each other. In the case of generalized developmental delay, academic skills, concentration, emotional and social development and even physical development may all be at the upper level of what is realistic to expect, regardless of the child or adolescent's actual, chronological age. An individualized intervention program will be warranted across all areas.

- If assessment results show an uneven pattern of maturity, build on areas where development is progressing well and provide specific intervention in areas where delays are noted. It is possible that an underlying disorder such as an Anxiety Disorder or Specific Learning Difficulty will have been identified.

Recommended further reading for immaturity

Building Resilience in Children and Teens: Giving Kids Roots and Wings
Author: Kenneth R. Ginsburg
Date of publication: 2011
Publisher: American Academy of Pediatrics

Child Development, 6th Edition
Author: Robert S. Feldman
Date of publication: 2011
Publisher: Pearson

Early Childhood Development and Its Variations
Authors: Kristine Slentz and Suzanne Krogh
Date of publication: 2001
Publisher: Routledge

How the Child's Mind Develops
Author: David Cohen
Date of publication: 2018
Publisher: Routledge

Resilient Children
Authors: Pam Farkas, Jerry Binder and Barrie Richter
Date of publication: 2011
Publisher: Pam Farkas, Jerry Binder and Barrie Richter

The Everything Parent's Guide to Emotional Intelligence in Children: How to Raise Children Who Are Caring, Resilient, and Emotionally Strong

Author: Korrel Kanoy
Date of publication: 2013
Publisher: Adams Media

Understanding Child Development

Author: Sara Meadows
Date of publication: 2018
Publisher: Routledge

Yardsticks: Children in the Classroom Ages 4–14

Author: Chip Wood
Date of publication: 2007
Publisher: Northeast Foundation for Children

Your Child from Six to Twelve

Author: Marion Faegre
Date of publication: 2010
Publisher: Sun Village Publications

Useful websites for immaturity

www.childdevelopmentinfo.com
Child Development Institute. Media organization
Information for parents and teachers. USA

www.raisingchildren.net.au
Raising Children Network. Government supported organization
Information for parents and teachers. Australia

www.kidsmatter.edu.au
Kids Matter. Government service
Information for parents and teachers. Australia

References for immaturity

Bowes, L. et al. (2010) 'Families promote emotional and behavioural resilience to bullying: evidence of an environmental effect', *Journal of Child Psychology and Psychiatry*, 51, pp. 809–817.

Dan, B. and Chéron, G. (2005) 'Developmental impairment that is not immaturity', *Developmental Medicine & Child Neurology*, 47, pp. 141–143.

Graziano, P.A., Keane, S.P. and Calkins, S.D. (2010) 'Maternal behaviour and children's early emotion regulation skills differentially predict development of children's reactive control and later effortful control', *Infant and Child Development*, 19, pp. 333–353.

Halldner, L. et al. (2014) 'Relative immaturity and ADHD', *Journal of Child Psychology and Psychiatry*, 55(8), pp. 897–904.

Klimstra, T.A. et al. (2012) 'Hypermaturity and immaturity of personality profiles in adolescents', *European Journal of Personality*, 26, pp. 203–211.

O'Brien, M. (2005) 'Enhancing early emotional development: guiding parents of young children', *Infant Mental Health Journal*, 26, pp. 284–286.

O'Connor, E. et al. (2011) 'Risks and outcomes associated with disorganized/controlling patterns of attachment at age three years in the National Institute of Child Health & Human Development Study of Early Child Care and Youth Development', *Infant Mental Health Journal*, 32, pp. 450–472.

Rees, C. (2012) 'Children's attachments', *Paediatrics and Child Health*, 22(5), pp. 186–192.

Ungar, M., Ghazinour, M. and Richter, J. (2013) 'What is resilience within the social ecology of human development?' *Journal of Child Psychology and Psychiatry*, 54, pp. 348–366.

Wachs, T.D. (2006) 'Contributions of temperament to buffering and sensitization processes in children's development', *Annals of the New York Academy of Sciences*, 1094, pp. 28–39.

Worcester, J. (2005) 'Pathways to competence: encouraging healthy social and emotional development in young children', *Infant Mental Health Journal*, 26, pp. 85–87.

LOW SELF-ESTEEM CHECKLIST

Glynis Hannell BA (Hons) MSc Psychologist

Name of child or adolescent   Age

Each item should be checked off using the following rating scale

0   Not at all, never occurs, does not apply
1   Mild, sometimes observed, applies to some extent
2   Moderate, often observed, certainly applies
3   Severe, frequently observed, strongly applies

Unrealistic perceptions about self

Says negative things about themselves	0	1	2	3
Exaggerates or fabricates stories to inflate own image	0	1	2	3
Does not expect to be liked	0	1	2	3
Does not expect to succeed	0	1	2	3

Weak foundations for positive self-esteem

Learning difficulties	0	1	2	3
Social difficulties	0	1	2	3
Clumsy, poor at physical skills	0	1	2	3

Not confident with schoolwork

Unwilling to try new things unless sure of success	0	1	2	3
Does not initiate own learning	0	1	2	3
Unwilling to take on extra or more challenging tasks	0	1	2	3
Avoids answering in class	0	1	2	3

Does not cope well with failure

Says 'I don't know' or 'I can't remember' to avoid errors	0	1	2	3
Gets upset if they lose	0	1	2	3
Argues things are not fair when they fail	0	1	2	3
Reluctant to try again if they have failed at something	0	1	2	3
Blames bad luck or others for failure	0	1	2	3
Exaggerates failures when they do occur	0	1	2	3
Reluctant to ask for help when in difficulty	0	1	2	3
Devalues the success of others	0	1	2	3

Does not cope well with success

Brags and 'goes over the top' when they succeed	0	1	2	3
Uncomfortable with praise or compliments	0	1	2	3
Attributes success to good luck	0	1	2	3

Finds it hard to accept responsibility for own actions

Denies wrongdoing even when clearly at fault 0 1 2 3
Unwilling to make decisions, wants someone else to decide........................0 1 2 3
Finds it difficult to apologize 0 1 2 3

Negative perceptions from others

Put down by siblings and/or peers 0 1 2 3
Put down by adults in family or community..0 1 2 3
Victim of teasing or bullying...0 1 2 3

Easily led

Anxious to follow peer group fads and fashions..0 1 2 3
Easily led by others...0 1 2 3
Does not initiate activities...0 1 2 3
Does not voice own opinion 0 1 2 3

Image is very important

Tries to look tough, tries to maintain a 'cool' image 0 1 2 3
Tries to impress peers by acting the clown 0 1 2 3
Uses possessions to gain prestige 0 1 2 3

Does not have positive friendships

Bullies younger or weaker children 0 1 2 3
Associates with peers who are unpopular with others.................................0 1 2 3
Tries to buy friendships 0 1 2 3

Eating patterns disturbed

Tries to improve image by extreme dieting 0 1 2 3
Eats for comfort..0 1 2 3

Positive characteristics and strengths (describe at least 3)

Important notes

This checklist can be used to help recognize low self-esteem. However, several conditions have similar characteristics and there may a range of explanations for the observations made. Specialist assessment is necessary for a formal diagnosis.

- Supporting notes on low self-esteem (pages 162–7)

- Guides for discussions with colleagues, parents and students (pages 184–8)

SUPPORTING NOTES ON LOW SELF-ESTEEM

Characteristics of low self-esteem

Low self-esteem is not a disorder or a disease. However, it can have a marked impact on social relationships, behaviour, emotional wellbeing and academic progress.

Low self-esteem is associated with feelings of personal inadequacy. The child or adolescent may believe that they are less competent or less likely to succeed than others and more likely to fail or to disappoint. Low self-esteem is also reflected in a sense of being less deserving than others of love, friendship, respect, fairness or success.

It is important to remember that self-esteem relates to a subjective evaluation of self-worth. It is not unusual for objective proof of competence and success to co-exist with subjective feelings of worthlessness and inadequacy.

Low self-esteem often brings with it distorted beliefs about the cause of success and failure. Successes are attributed to 'luck' and failures blamed on personal inadequacy. Motivation can be limited by expectations of failure and a sense of fatalism regarding success. Sometimes a sense of personal inadequacy may be disguised by behaviour intended to impress others such as bragging, acts of bravado and so on.

Causes of low self-esteem

Temperament and personality are to some extent genetically determined and in turn it is likely that a predisposition to low self-esteem has a genetic trace. A tendency to be a perfectionist with a high drive to succeed may set up the beginnings of low self-esteem; a pessimistic temperament may underpin negative judgments about personal achievements or self-worth.

Parenting style, family and community values and life experiences can contribute to the development of both positive and negative self-esteem. Low self-esteem is also associated with chronic ill health and obesity. Experiencing difficulties with concentration, learning or socialization can also have a damaging effect on self-esteem.

Other people's behaviour can contribute to loss of self-esteem. A parent or teacher may be constantly and inappropriately critical, and siblings or peers may harass, ridicule, tease and damage self-esteem. Sexual, physical or emotional abuse is likely to have a major impact on self-esteem.

Conditions which may be mistaken for low self-esteem

Depression

Depression and low self-esteem are very closely connected and there is often significant overlap. If Depression is the primary underlying disorder, then self-esteem can be expected to improve once Depression has been treated or has spontaneously resolved.

Conditions which may occur alongside low self-esteem

Low self-esteem with Specific Learning Disorders

Difficulties and failures in the classroom can bring frustration, social stigma and Low self-esteem.

Low self-esteem with Attention-Deficit Disorder

Impulsive, inattentive behaviour, social difficulties and poor academic performance may bring constant criticism and punishment and a strong message of failure and inadequacy.

Low self-esteem with maltreatment, abuse and bullying

Low self-esteem is a very common consequence of being sexually, physically, or mentally abused. Abuse of any kind reinforces the concept that the victim is worthless and undeserving of affection or respect. In addition, abusers and bullies often select victims with low self-esteem as they are more vulnerable and less able to stand up for themselves.

Low self-esteem with Depression

These two conditions can coexist or can mimic each other. Expert clinical judgment is required to diagnose and treat symptoms of Depression and low self-esteem.

Professionals supporting the student

Teachers

Teachers will have the primary duty of care in school. Teachers with specialist expertise may offer programs to develop self-affirmation, self-respect and appropriate social skills.

Counsellors

School counsellors may offer personal counselling and support.

Social workers

Social workers will be involved in cases of inadequate parenting, abuse or a dysfunctional family.

Psychiatrists and psychologists

Psychiatrists and psychologists may be consulted for specialist intervention.

Strategies for meeting the student's needs (low self-esteem)

General strategies for meeting the student's needs (low self-esteem)

- Identify any social factors contributing to low self-esteem such as bullying, abuse, inappropriate parenting or teaching styles and so on and deal with these issues as appropriate.

- Identify any learning or concentration difficulties which may be contributing to low self-esteem and introduce appropriate, positive support.

- Identify any physical factors such as obesity, ill health or poor coordination which may be contributing to low self-esteem and arrange for appropriate management.

- Avoid 'blanket praise'. Overuse of phrases such as 'good job', 'amazing', 'fantastic' destroys the value of praise. Make praise fairly difficult to earn so that it has value when it is given.

- Be sincere when you praise. Explain what you like about the behaviour or work that you are praising. For example, 'Jack this is excellent work, you used proper sentences for every answer, well done'.

- Value effort and attitude rather than outcomes. Not everyone can write a great story, but everyone can give their best effort.

- When there is a need for discipline, use face-saving strategies which suggest you have confidence in them. Give them a chance to redeem themselves. 'I'll bet you can tell me which rule you forgot' or 'What's the best way out of this one Paul?' instead of 'How many times have I told you not to do that?' or 'I can't trust you to do anything right'.

- Attribute success and failure honestly and teach the child or adolescent to do the same.

- Give credit for effort if that has led to success. 'You made your own luck by the way you stuck at it'.

- Acknowledge ability when it is on show, 'Just look at the way you used those interesting words, it really lifted it to a top piece of work'.

- Attribute failure honestly; if they could have done better let them acknowledge this: 'Kyle, tell me three things you'd do better if you did this piece of work over again'.

- If they have done their best, move the blame from them; it was not their fault. 'That was a tough one, full marks for giving it a try'.

- Use biographies, stories, and guest speakers from your community to show that everyone has a unique contribution to make and can overcome setbacks and limitations.

- Celebrate positive personal qualities such as kindness, cheerfulness, truthfulness, commonsense, helpfulness, persistence and so on as well as academic achievements.

- Express warm feelings, genuine interest and make it personal: 'Shar, can I take it to show it to the other teachers?' or 'Eli, it's great to see you back'. Remember that your body language speaks as loudly as your words.

- Showcase individual interests and strengths.

- Being a peer tutor, buddy or leader to younger children can build self-esteem so provide opportunities for this type of activity.

- Use concepts such as 'personal best' and 'most improved' as well as absolute scores to recognize achievements.

- Personalize the classroom so that individual names are mentioned and credited in many ways: 'Neat library brought to you by Chaz and Liah', or 'Personal best for writing Ben, Josh and Han'.

Recommended further reading for low self-esteem

Challenging the Cult of Self-esteem in Education

Author: Kenzo Bergeron
Date of publication: 2018
Publisher: Routledge

Cool, Calm and Confident

Author: Lisa Schab
Date of publication: 2009
Publisher: Instant Help Books

I'm Gonna Like Me: Letting Off a Little Self-Esteem

Authors: Jamie Lee Curtis and Laura Cornell
Date of publication: 2007
Publisher: Harper Collins Publishers

Ollie and His Super Powers

Author: Alison Knowles
Date of publication: 2016
Publisher: Jessica Kingsley

Self-Esteem and Children: How to Build Self-esteem in kids

Author: Raz Miller
Date of publication: 2013
Publisher: Amazon Digital Services

Talkabout for Children 1. Developing Self-Awareness and Self-Esteem, 2nd Edition

Author: Alex Kelly
Date of publication: 2018
Publisher: Routledge

The Self-Esteem Trap: Raising Confident and Compassionate Kids in an Age of Self-Importance

Author: Polly Young-Eisendrath
Date of publication: 2009
Publisher: Little, Brown and Company

The Turned-Off Child: Learned Helplessness and School Failure

Authors: Myrna Gordon and Robert Gordon
Date of publication: 2012
Publisher: Myrna Gordon

Useful websites for low self-esteem

www.childdevelopmentinfo.com
Child Development Institute. Media organization
Information for parents and teachers. USA

www.raisingchildren.net.au
Raising Children Network. Government supported organization
Information for parents and teachers. Australia
www.kidsmatter.edu.au

Kids Matter. Government service
Information for parents and teachers. Australia

www.youngminds.org.uk
Young Minds. Not for profit organization
Information for parents, teachers and young people. UK

References for low self-esteem

Ajilchi, B., Borjali, A. and Janbozorgi, M. (2011) 'The impact of a parenting skills training program on stressed mothers and their children's self-esteem level', *Procedia – Social and Behavioral Sciences*, 30, pp. 316–326.

Chan, S.M. and Wong, A.K.Y. (2013) 'Shyness in late childhood: relations with attributional styles and self-esteem', *Child: Care, Health and Development*, 39, pp. 213–219.

Doumen, S. et al. (2011) 'Teacher–child conflict and aggressive behaviour in first grade: the intervening role of children's self-esteem', *Infant and Child Development*, 20, pp. 449–465.

Ek, U. et al. (2008) 'Self-esteem in children with attention and/or learning deficits: the importance of gender', *Acta Paediatrica*, 97, pp. 1125–1130.

Flouri, E. (2006) 'Parental interest in children's education, children's self-esteem and locus of control, and later educational attainment: twenty-six year follow-up of the 1970 British birth cohort', *British Journal of Educational Psychology*, 76, pp. 41–55.

Gruenenfelder-Steiger, A. et al. (2016) 'Subjective and objective peer approval evaluations and self-esteem development', *Developmental Psychology*, 52(10), pp. 1563–1577.

Lehman, B.J. and Repetti, R.L. (2007) 'Bad days don't end when the school bell rings: the lingering effects of negative school events on children's mood, self-esteem, and perceptions of parent–child interaction', *Social Development*, 16, pp. 596–618.

Määttä, S., Nurmi, J.-E. and Stattin, H. (2007) 'Achievement orientations, school adjustment, and well-being: a longitudinal study', *Journal of Research on Adolescence*, 17, pp. 789–812.

Mărgăriţoiu, A. and Eftimie, S. (2012) 'Abused children's self-esteem', *Procedia – Social and Behavioral Sciences*, 46, pp. 4580–4584.

Miller, D., Topping, K. and Thurston, A. (2010) 'Peer tutoring in reading: the effects of role and organization on two dimensions of self-esteem', *British Journal of Educational Psychology*, 80, pp. 417–433.

Pinquart, M. (2013) 'Self-esteem of children and adolescents with chronic illness: a meta-analysis', *Child: Care, Health and Development*, 39, pp. 153–161.

Rose, C. et al. (2017) 'Bully perpetration and self-esteem', *Behavioral Disorders*, 42(4), pp. 159–169.

Taylor, A. et al. (2012) 'Self-esteem and body dissatisfaction in young children: associations with weight and perceived parenting style', *Clinical Psychologist*, 16, pp. 25–35.

Thomaes, S. et al. (2010) 'I like me if you like me: on the interpersonal modulation and regulation of preadolescents' state of self-esteem', *Child Development*, 81, pp. 811–825.

Thomson, M.M. (2012) 'Labelling and self-esteem: does labelling exceptional students impact their self-esteem?' *Support for Learning*, 27, pp. 158–165.

CHAPTER 7

Sensory

Impairments in hearing or vision range from mild to severe. Although severe impairments are often picked up in early infancy, mild difficulties may go unnoticed for many years. Obviously, this can significantly impact on the child's development, particularly within the classroom.

All senses rely on a receptive mechanism, such as eyes and ears to receive stimulation directly from the environment. Problems with the physical structures of the eyes or ears will of course impair the way the child or adolescent sees or hears.

However, neurological networks that transmit and process the sensory information within the brain are also a major cause of impairments in vision or hearing.

Both hearing and visual impairments can occur singly or together. They may occur where a child has multiple disabilities such as concurrently occurring Intellectual Disability, Cerebral Palsy, Hearing Impairment and Visual Impairment.

This chapter contains two checklists relating to sensory impairments.

HEARING IMPAIRMENT CHECKLIST

Glynis Hannell BA (Hons) MSc Psychologist

Name of child or adolescent   Age

Each item should be checked off using the following rating scale

0   Not at all, never occurs, does not apply
1   Mild, sometimes observed, applies to some extent
2   Moderate, often observed, certainly applies
3   Severe, frequently observed, strongly applies

Difficulties in hearing sound

Does not turn towards sounds 0	1	2	3
Does not respond to speech when not able to see the speaker..................0	1	2	3
Fails to notice when their name is called 0	1	2	3
Fails to notice noises such as buzzer or bell 0	1	2	3
Confuses words of similar sound such as *Jesus/cheeses*...........................0	1	2	3
Often says 'I didn't hear you' 0	1	2	3
Difficulties hearing against background noise..0	1	2	3

Difficulties in understanding what is said

Misunderstands what is said. 0	1	2	3
Difficulties following instructions 0	1	2	3
Asks people to repeat what they have said 0	1	2	3

Listening behaviour suggests hearing problems

Watches speaker's face when listening 0	1	2	3
Tilts head to listen...0	1	2	3
Sits very close to the teacher or the television 0	1	2	3
Watches others and copies them when instructions are given 0	1	2	3
Seems in a world of his or her own at times 0	1	2	3
Turns up volume of TV, audio...0	1	2	3

Spoken language shows signs of hearing difficulties

Pronounces words incorrectly such as *eagle/equal* 0	1	2	3
Speaks more loudly than is necessary..0	1	2	3
Speech is difficult to understand...0	1	2	3

Positive characteristics and strengths (describe at least 3)

Important notes

This checklist can be used to help diagnose and recognize Hearing Impairment. However, several conditions have similar characteristics and there may a range of explanations for the observations made. Specialist assessment is necessary for a formal diagnosis.

- Supporting notes on Hearing Impairment (pages 171–5)
- Guides for discussions with colleagues, parents and students (pages 184–8)

SUPPORTING NOTES ON HEARING IMPAIRMENT
Characteristics of Hearing Impairment

A Hearing Impairment may occur in only one ear (unilateral) or in both ears (bilateral). Hearing may be affected across all frequencies of sounds. The impairment can range from mild through to profound. Serious Hearing Impairments will usually have been identified through screening at preschool level or after an accident or illness such as meningitis or measles.

However mild or recently occurring hearing difficulties may not have been picked up. In the case of severely or multiply disabled children Hearing Impairments are more likely to occur and may possibly have been overlooked.

There are three main types of hearing loss referred to as sensori-neural, conductive and central hearing loss.

Disorders of the middle ear are generally responsible for conductive losses; disorders of the cochlea or cochlear nerve are generally responsible for sensorineural hearing loss; and disorders of the brainstem or brain are generally responsible for central hearing loss.

Sometimes only certain frequencies of sound are affected. Gaps will then occur in the perception of speech depending on the frequency for which hearing is impaired.

For instance, if there is a hearing loss in high frequencies then some consonant sounds (particularly *f, s* and *th, sh and ch*, and maybe *k* and *t*) may be lost and the sentence becomes meaningless. 'Sue is going to have a shower' may be heard as 'Ue i going to have a owner'. If the loss is in the lower frequencies, then lower frequency vowel sounds may not be perceived.

Hearing Impairments can significantly impact on the development of both receptive and expressive language and related skills. Hearing difficulties are associated with a higher risk of language, academic, social and behavioural difficulties.

Even after surgery or the provision of hearing aids hearing may still be impaired, but to a lesser degree than before. The specialist's advice will help parents and teachers to understand the particular constellation of hearing difficulties experienced by an individual who has been treated for a Hearing Impairment.

In the case of mild, intermittent or transitory Hearing Impairments, language, learning and socialization may be negatively affected.

Causes of Hearing Impairment

Hearing Impairments can be hereditary with a family pattern of similar hearing loss.

Maternal infections including rubella (German Measles), prematurity or birth complications can result in a Hearing Impairment.

Craniofacial abnormalities, an adverse reaction to certain medications or childhood illnesses such as meningitis, mumps or measles can also damage hearing.

Hearing can also be damaged by injuries, by persistent ear infections or perforated eardrums. We also know that other developmental disorders, particularly Intellectual Disability, bring with them a higher than expected incidence of Hearing Impairment.

Hearing Impairments can significantly impact on the development of both receptive and expressive language and related skills and are associated with a higher risk of academic, social and behavioural difficulties.

Conditions which may be mistaken for Hearing Impairment

Speech or Language Disorder

Problems with receptive language and/or expressive language can give the impression that hearing is impaired. For example, a child may hear a sentence perfectly well, but because of a Language Disorder not respond or understand what is said. Or a child with a Speech Disorder may sound as if they have a Hearing Impairment when they do not.

Selective Mutism

Children with Selective Mutism may give the appearance that they have not heard.

Auditory Processing Disorder (APD)

There is still considerable professional debate about what, if anything, constitutes APD, or Central Auditory Processing Disorder (CAPD) as it is sometimes called. As yet there are no diagnostic criteria that are universally accepted to explain and categorize observed difficulties in processing auditory information in the absence of a diagnosed Hearing Impairment.

Conditions which may occur alongside Hearing Impairment

Hearing Impairment with Intellectual Disability

There is clear research evidence that Hearing Impairments are much more prevalent in children and adolescents with an Intellectual Disability than in the general population. In the case of severe or multiple disabilities it is not uncommon for a Hearing Impairment to have been overlooked.

Hearing Impairment with Visual Impairment

Sadly, there are a number of conditions where both hearing and vision are impaired. Maternal rubella was in the past a major cause of this condition. This has now reduced due to vaccination, and extreme prematurity is now the leading cause of congenital deaf-blindness in infants. A genetically transmitted condition called Usher Syndrome accounts for most other cases of childhood deaf-blindness.

Professionals supporting the student (Hearing Impairment)

Teachers and special educators

The team of professionals at school, including class teacher, special education coordinator and teaching staff, teaching assistants and school leaders will be involved in providing an appropriate, inclusive program.

Otolaryngologist (ear, nose and throat specialist) and/or otologist/neurotologist

They will provide specialist diagnosis and treatment such as surgery, cochlear implants and so on.

Audiologist

An audiologist will assess hearing and arrange for hearing aids and other assistive technology.

Speech therapist

A speech therapist will provide ongoing input for verbal communication, or a specialist signing teacher may teach signing if this is selected as the best way to establish communication.

Specialist organizations

There are often organizations offering specialist information, special programs and family support in local areas.

Strategies for meeting the student's needs (Hearing Impairment)

Strategies for specialist advice and monitoring

- Appropriate diagnostic testing and treatment should be provided.
- Regular reviews of hearing by appropriate specialists should be standard practice.
- Specialist advice should be made available to the parents and the teachers regarding the impact of the Hearing Impairment with and without aids. Specialists can also advise on appropriate strategies in the classroom and at home.
- Equipment such as hearing aids and radio loops need to be properly maintained and checked regularly.
- Speech and language therapy may be required and may involve teaching staff at school.

Strategies for the classroom

- Every effort should be made to provide the best listening environment possible, for example carpeted areas, acoustic ceiling tiles and a quiet location away from traffic or busy areas of the school can all help to reduce ambient noise.
- Background noises in the classroom should be kept to a minimum. Classroom fish tanks, heating or cooling systems, and outside noises should be monitored and attenuated as far as possible.
- Use of a closed loop sound system in the classroom which operates through hearing aids can be very successful for some individuals with Hearing Impairment.

- Use of a surround-sound system where the teacher's voice is transmitted to speakers throughout the classroom significantly enhances everyone's ability to hear and focus on what the teacher is saying.

Strategies for listening

- Seating should be close to the teacher and face on.
- When speaking one to one the teacher should avoid speaking from the side or from behind, face-to-face is much better.
- Supplement verbal communication with facial expression and gesture.
- Supplement verbal communication with written lesson notes, diagrams and illustrations.
- The teacher's face should be well lit when speaking to the class or to the individual with a Hearing Impairment.
- Give clear signals when listening is going to be required and make sure that you have their attention.
- Give clear signals when listening is not going to be required, so that there is no need for effortful listening 'just in case' something important is said.

General strategies

- Recognize that even mild Hearing Impairments can make each day more frustrating and exhausting than would otherwise be the case. Allow for rest and respite from the need to listen or speak if this proves to be helpful.
- View behavioural and social problems as possible consequences of Hearing Impairment and deal with accordingly.
- Arrange for a buddy system so that there is extra support within the classroom and during recreation breaks.
- In the case of severely or multiply disabled children or adolescents, ensure that hearing has, as far as possible, been checked.
- If signing is used ensure that teachers, teaching aids and peers learn to sign.

Recommended further reading for Hearing Impairment

Helping Deaf and Hard of Hearing Students to Use Spoken Language: A Guide for Educators and Families

Authors: Susan Easterbrooks and Ellen Estes

Date of publication: 2007

Publisher: Corwin Press

Literacy Instruction for Students who are Deaf and Hard of Hearing (Professional Perspectives on Deafness: Evidence and Applications)

Authors: Susan Easterbrooks and Jennifer Beal-Alvarez

Date of publication: 2013

Publisher: Oxford University Press

Teaching Students with Sensory Disabilities. A Practical Guide for Every Teacher

Author: Robert Algozzine

Date of publication: 2006

Publisher: Corwin Press

Useful websites for Hearing Impairment

www. deafchildren.org

American Society for Deaf Children. Not for profit organization

Information for parents and teachers. USA

www.ndcs.org.uk

National Deaf Children's Society. Not for profit organization

Information for parents and teachers. UK

www.ridbc.org.au

Royal Institute for Deaf and Blind Children. Not for profit organization

Information for parents and teachers. Australia

References for Hearing Impairment

American Psychiatric Association (2013) *Diagnostic and Statistical Manual of Mental Disorders, 5th Edition*, Washington, DC: APA.

Barr, E. et al. (2007) 'The prevalence of ENT disorders in pre-school children with Down Syndrome', *Clinical Otolaryngology*, 32, pp. 510–515.

Dawes, P. and Bishop, D. (2009) 'Auditory processing disorder in relation to developmental disorders of language, communication and attention: a review and critique', *International Journal of Language & Communication Disorders*, 44, pp. 440–465.

Eleweke, C.J. et al. (2008) 'Information about support services for families of young children with hearing loss: a review of some useful outcomes and challenges', *Deafness Education. International*, 10, pp. 190–212.

Engel-Yeger, B. et al. (2013) 'Comparing participation in out of school activities between children with visual impairments, children with hearing impairments and typical peers', *Research in Developmental Disabilities*, 10, pp. 3124–3132.

Fitzpatrick, E. et al. (2017) 'Exploring reasons for late identification of children with early onset hearing loss', *International Journal of Pediatric Otorhinolaryngology*, 100, pp. 107–113.

Hild, U. et al. (2008) 'High prevalence of hearing disorders at the Special Olympics indicate need to screen persons with intellectual disability', *Journal of Intellectual Disability Research*, 52, pp. 520–528.

Hogan, A. et al. (2011) 'Communication and behavioural disorders among children with hearing loss increases risk of mental health disorders', *Australian and New Zealand Journal of Public Health*, 35, pp. 377–383.

Kretschmer, L.W. and Kretschmer, R.R. (2010) 'Intervention for children with auditory or visual sensory impairments', in Damico, J.S., Müller, N. and Ball, M.J. (Eds), *The Handbook of Language and Speech Disorders*, Oxford, UK: Wiley-Blackwell.

Maerlender, A. (2010) 'Short-term memory and auditory processing disorders: concurrent validity and clinical diagnostic markers', *Psychology in Schools*, 47, pp. 975–984.

Marriage, J. et al. (2018) 'Hearing Impairment in children', *Paediatrics and Child Health*, 27, pp. 441–446.

Peterson, C.C. and Wellman, H.M. (2009) 'From fancy to reason: scaling deaf and hearing children's understanding of theory of mind and pretence', *British Journal of Developmental Psychology*, 27, pp. 297–310.

Stevenson, J. et al. (2010) 'The relationship between language development and behaviour problems in children with hearing loss', *Journal of Child Psychology and Psychiatry*, 51, pp. 77–83.

World Health Organization (2007) *ICIDH-2: International Classification of Functioning, Disability and Health – Children and Youth*, Geneva: WHO.

VISUAL IMPAIRMENT CHECKLIST

Glynis Hannell BA (Hons) MSc Psychologist

Name of child or adolescent   Age

Each item should be checked off using the following rating scale

0   Not at all, never occurs, does not apply
1   Mild, sometimes observed, applies to some extent
2   Moderate, often observed, certainly applies
3   Severe, frequently observed, strongly applies

General visual difficulties

Complains of headaches or difficulties seeing 0	1	2	3
Leaves words out when reading or copying 0	1	2	3
Confuses similar shapes such as 3 and 8 0	1	2	3
Makes mistakes with colours 0	1	2	3
Messy bookwork.....0	1	2	3
Bumps into things, poor at ball games.....0	1	2	3

Sign of difficulties with close work

Holds books very close or keeps shifting position 0	1	2	3
Looks sideways or squints at print 0	1	2	3
Leans back when reading or writing.....0	1	2	3
Puts head very near the desk when working.....0	1	2	3
Tilts head to one side when writing or drawing 0	1	2	3
Loses place when reading or copying; skips lines.....0	1	2	3

Signs of difficulties with distance work

Squints, frowns or leans forward when copying from the board.....0	1	2	3
Tilts head when trying to see in the distance 0	1	2	3
Copies from students sitting nearby instead of copying from the board 0	1	2	3
Sits close to the television or board 0	1	2	3

Physical problems with eyes

Eyes do not coordinate; move in different directions.....0	1	2	3
Eyes flicker or seem to drift.....0	1	2	3
Sensitive to bright light 0	1	2	3
Red eyes, itchiness or discomfort 0	1	2	3
Eyes water very easily 0	1	2	3
Pupils of eyes are different from one another in size 0	1	2	3
Pupil of eye is white or cloudy.....0	1	2	3

Positive characteristics and strengths (describe at least 3)

Important notes

This checklist can be used to help diagnose and recognize visual impairment. However, several conditions have similar characteristics and there may a range of explanations for the observations made. Specialist assessment is necessary for a formal diagnosis.

● Supporting notes on Visual Impairment (pages 177–80)
● Guides for discussions with colleagues, parents and students (pages 184–8)

SUPPORTING NOTES ON VISUAL IMPAIRMENT

Characteristics of Visual Impairment

Many visual problems do not have any outward signs of difficulties and parents or teachers may be unaware of any problems. Of course, severe visual impairment is usually picked up early on in life and regular eye sight checks will pick up most other visual difficulties.

However, nowadays children's eyesight is not always checked regularly, meaning that there is a high risk of some children having undetected visual problems. There are various forms of visual impairment.

Amblyopia is sometimes called 'lazy eye'. In this condition there is usually a difference in acuity (sharpness of vision) between the two eyes or poor coordination between the movements of the two eyes. To avoid having to deal with conflicting information from the two eyes the brain ignores the messages from the weaker eye and stops developing nerve connections to it. If left untreated amblyopia can cause permanent loss of sight in the weaker eye. This loss is usually permanent by the age of about 10.

Strabismus is sometimes referred to as 'a squint'. This is a condition where the eyes do not line up with each other, with one eye turning in, out, up or down. This may cause amblyopia (see above).

Refractive errors are problems with the focus of the visual image which result in blurred vision. Astigmatism makes objects up close and at a distance appear blurry. Hyperopia causes objects up close appear out of focus whereas myopia causes distant objects to appear out of focus. Myopia is the most common form of visual problem seen in school age children. Each eye may have a different ability to focus and this may cause amblyopia (see above).

Causes of Visual Impairment

Good vision depends on both eyes focusing well and coordinating with each other to successfully transfer visual signals to an area of the brain called the visual cortex, where the signals are coordinated and interpreted. Genetic or congenital factors can impact on the normal development of any part of this visual system. Extreme prematurity can lead to damage of the retina, and illnesses such as measles and rubella can also damage parts of the eye. In developing countries, Vitamin A deficiency is a major cause of visual impairment. In many parts of the world amblyopia (referred to above) is a major cause of loss of vision in one eye.

The most common causes of mild to moderate visual impairment are refractive errors, where the natural shape of the eye is elongated (myopia), shortened (hyperopia) or where the there is an irregular curvature of the cornea or the lens (astigmatism). Strabismus is also congenital. Whilst there is a genetic component in refractive errors there is also research evidence to suggest that myopia increases in urbanized environments and with increased education and decreases when more time is spent outdoors.

Conditions which may be mistaken for Visual Impairment

There are no other conditions which could readily be mistaken for Visual Impairment.

Conditions which may occur alongside Visual Impairment

Visual Impairment with Hearing Impairment

Sadly, there are a number of conditions where both vision and hearing are impaired. Maternal rubella used to be a major cause of this condition. This has now reduced due to vaccination and extreme prematurity is now the leading cause of congenital deaf-blindness in infants. A genetically transmitted condition called Usher Syndrome accounts for most other cases of childhood deaf-blindness.

Visual impairment with multiple developmental disabilities

Visual impairment occurs very frequently in tandem with other developmental disabilities. Approximately 50% of multiply disabled children have a visual impairment.

Professionals supporting the student (Visual Impairment)

Teachers and special educators

The team of professionals at school, including class teacher, special education coordinator and teaching staff, teaching assistants and school leaders will be involved in providing an appropriate, inclusive program.

Optometrists (also called ophthalmic opticians)

Optometrists are professionals who examine eyes for defects, diagnose problems and prescribe corrective lenses or other treatment. Opticians fit and adjust glasses.

Ophthalmologists

Ophthalmologists are medical doctors who specialize in the diagnosis and treatment of eye disorders and diseases.

Specialist organizations

There are often organizations offering specialist information, special programs and family support in local areas.

Strategies for meeting the student's needs (Visual Impairment)

Strategies for specialist advice and monitoring

- Eyesight tests should be arranged. In most countries these are available at no or low cost for children, either through the school or public health system.
- Regular reviews of eyesight by appropriate specialists should be standard practice.

- Specialist advice should be made available to the parents and teachers, for example whether prescription lenses should be worn at all times or only in specific situations.

- Specialist advice should also be sought on any continuing limitations to vision which remain despite corrective lenses or treatment.

- Advice should be sought on appropriate management within the classroom. This might include the use of assistive devices such as a hand-held or stand magnifier, a slanted book rest for bringing things closer or at a better angle, bold lined paper, bold markers, large print and/or speaking calculator, computer software that magnifies information on the screen, text-to-voice software, video magnifier, CCTV and so on.

Strategies for the classroom

- Check that all areas are well lit, without shadows or reflected light.

- Avoid using coloured markers and chalks that are hard to see against the background.

- Make sure all curriculum materials are well presented with clear, sharp print.

- Avoid cramped, handwritten worksheets or poor quality photocopies.

- Seating should be close to the teacher and face on. Avoid seating positions which require turning or twisting to see the teacher or board.

- Supervise the use of spectacles for younger children to make sure they are worn appropriately.

General strategies

- Recognize that spectacles do not necessarily result in perfect vision.

- Recognize that even mild visual impairments can make each day more frustrating and exhausting than would otherwise be the case.

- View behavioural and learning problems as possible consequences of visual impairment and deal with accordingly.

- In the case of severely or multiply disabled children or adolescents, ensure that vision has, as far as possible, been checked.

Recommended further reading for Visual Impairment

Including Children with Visual Difficulties

Authors: Julie Jennings and Clare Beswick
Date of publication: 2009
Publisher: Featherstone Education

Including Children with Visual Impairments in Mainstream Schools. A Practical Guide

Author: Pauline Davis
Date of publication: 2003
Publisher: Routledge

Teaching Pupils with Visual Impairment. A Guide to Making the School Curriculum Accessible

Author: Ruth Salisbury

Date of publication: 2007

Publisher: Routledge

Teaching Students with Sensory Disabilities. A Practical Guide for Every Teacher

Author: Robert Algozzine

Date of publication: 2006

Publisher: Corwin Press

Visual Impairment. Access to Education for Children and Young People

Authors: Heather Mason and Stephen McCall

Date of publication: 2012

Publisher: Routledge

Useful websites for Visual Impairment

www.look-uk.org
Look. Not for profit organization
Information for parents. UK

www. nbcs.org.uk
National Blind Children's Association. Not for profit organization
Information for parents and teachers. UK

www.familyconnect.org
Family Connect. (Resource provided by the American Foundation for the Blind and National Association for Parents of Children with Visual Impairments.) Not for profit organization
Information for parents and teachers. USA

References for Visual Impairment

Engel-Yeger, B. et al. (2013) 'Comparing participation in out of school activities between children with visual impairments, children with hearing impairments and typical peers', *Research in Developmental Disabilities*, 10, pp. 3124–3132.

Fazzi, E. et al. (2007) 'Spectrum of visual disorders in children with Cerebral Visual Impairment', *Journal of Child Neurology*, 22(3), pp. 294–301.

Khadka, J. et al. (2012) 'Listening to voices of children with a visual impairment: a focus group study', *British Journal of Visual Impairment September*, 30, pp. 182–196.

Lueck, A. (2004) *Functional Vision: A Practitioner's Guide to Evaluation and Intervention*. New York, AFB Press.

Mackenzie, E.S and Hatton, D.D. (2013) 'Using repeated reading to improve reading speed and comprehension in students with visual impairments', *Journal of Visual Impairment and Blindness*, 107(2), pp. 93–106.

Pring, L. (2008) 'Psychological characteristics of children with visual impairments: learning, memory and imagery', *British Journal of Visual Impairment*, 26(2), pp. 159–169.

Rose, K. (2008) 'Time spent outdoors can prevent the development of myopia', *Acta Ophthalmologica*, 86, pp. 12–18.

Saw, S.M. et al. (2007) 'School grades and myopia', *Ophthalmic and Physiological Optics*, 27, pp. 126–129.

Spunqin, S. (2002) *When You Have a Visually Impaired Student in Your Classroom: A Guide for Teachers*, New York, AFB Press.

Theodorou, N. and Shipman, T. (2013) 'An overview of a UK paediatric visual impaired population and low vision aid provision', *British Journal of Visual Impairment*, 31, pp. 60–67.

World Health Organization (2007) *International Classification of Functioning, Disability and Health-Children and Youth Version*, Geneva: WHO.

Supplementary resources

The previous chapters in this book have provided checklists and supporting notes on 20 categories of special needs.

This final chapter provides some supplementary resources.

TRUSTWORTHY OR NOT?

Finding a reliable professional when you can pay for extra help.

All parents want the very best for their child, so it is natural for them to look for whatever help is available. These questions may help you check that any extra help you pay for is from a reputable provider.

What are your qualifications?

Ask what the letters after their name stand for. Look for Bachelor's or Master's degrees or doctorates in education, speech therapy, medicine etc from a reputable university. Letters such as BA, BSc, MA, MSc, or PhD are reassuring.

Be suspicious of diplomas and certificates from organizations other than universities. Be suspicious of long strings of letters after the person's name, they are often used to cover up a lack of academic qualifications.

What professional organizations do you belong to?

Look for organizations that have national or international standing, with professional websites giving comprehensive details of their organization, how they are funded, requirements for membership, conferences they run etc.

Be suspicious of organizations which do not provide much information about themselves or seem to be heavily marketing their services. Be suspicious of people who do not belong to any mainstream organizations.

How is your treatment different to what my child's school or hospital can provide?

Look for reassurance the treatment being offered is also available through the best schools and/or public health services. The only difference will be that you can pay to have immediate access to the service. In large cities expect to find several professionals offering a similar service.

Be suspicious if you are told the treatment is unique or not available elsewhere. Good treatments are usually taken up quickly by reputable private and public organizations around the world. Reputable professionals and organizations only avoid 'treatments' that don't work or which are dangerous.

Do I have to sign a contract with you? Can I stop the program at any time?

Look for an arrangement that you can stop at any time, without any further financial obligation.

Be suspicious of contracts that lock you into financial commitments. Be careful of 'hard sell' pressure to sign or stay with a program.

Can you provide some references to vouch for what you do?

Look for references from reputable people such as doctors, teachers and established organizations.

Be suspicious of claims of miracle cures or endorsements without the contact details of the person making the recommendation.

Do you have professional indemnity and public liability insurance?

Look for a clear 'yes'. This is for your protection if anything goes wrong.

Be suspicious if you are told these are not necessary or not in place.

How will we be able to tell if my child is making progress with you?

Look for a plan to track progress using tests, scores or measures that will be reported back to you. Look for measures that could be double checked by someone else.

Be suspicious if there is no clear plan to measure progress. Just promising progress is not good enough.

I would like to discuss your proposed treatment with my child's teacher/doctor. Can you give me some information to explain what you do and how it works?

Look for a positive response and willingness to provide information. An offer to speak directly to the teacher/doctor is a plus.

Be suspicious of attempts to avoid providing information or a suggestion that such contact is not needed.

Have you always had complete success with this treatment?

Look for an honest acknowledgement that there have been some disappointing results and/or failures with previous clients. Expect a reasonable explanation of the limits of the treatment.

Be suspicious of claims of 100% success with every previous client.

How long have you been in practice? Where did you work before?

Look for an established practice which has been in operation for a good length of time. In the case of a new practice, look for the person's previous relevant experience. They should have been doing similar work in a different setting before setting up their new service.

Be suspicious of new set ups where the person providing the service does not have previous experience in a very similar type of work.

What is the scientific basis for what you do? Are there text books or professional journal articles I could read?

Look for an informative reply and a willingness to give information about text books and/or professional journal articles. A competent professional should be able to name reliable journals without hesitation.

Be careful that the 'science' checks out. Unscrupulous operators can make up 'science' that sounds plausible but is, in fact, nonsense. Be suspicious if they cannot recommend text books or journal articles to support their claims. Check that books are serious reference books, not promotional material.

GUIDE: DISCUSSING A STUDENT'S SPECIAL NEEDS WITH COLLEAGUES

Busy professionals need to collaborate, tapping into the expertise and experience of everyone and sharing ideas to formulate the best way forward. The checklists in this book facilitate this by allowing everyone to consider the same questions about the student before coming to the discussion.

Meetings work best if the person convening the meeting has a clear 'road map' for the discussion ahead of time. Whether there is a formal agenda or not, an underlying structure makes a meeting much more successful.

No-one likes to waste time attending meetings. Some preparation ahead of time makes sure that every meeting makes the very best use of the time and expertise of those who attend.

Preparing for a meeting

- Purpose of the meeting. A clearly stated purpose helps to make a meeting productive and efficient. List the topics that need to be covered on the agenda.

- Who will attend? Ensure that all the key people attend, send a report or are represented.

- Who will lead the discussion? Choose sometime who can keep the discussion on track, deal firmly with time wasters and give everyone a fair say.

- Will attendees be asked to give a report at the meeting? Alert anyone who will be asked to report to the meeting so that they can come prepared.

- What questions should be raised? Suggested questions can be considered.

- What preparation needs to be done ahead of the meeting? Ask participants to prepare for the meeting, for example completing checklists, reading supporting notes, making phone calls to specialists.

- What documents need to be circulated ahead of time? Send out copies of documents that relate to the meeting ahead of time.

- How will the proceedings of the meeting be recorded? For small meetings a file note written by the convener may suffice. For more complex meetings appoint a competent minute taker

Discussion with colleagues – using the checklists

Which checklist items are the most important from our professional perspective?

What are the student's areas of greatest difficulty?

What positive characteristics or abilities can we focus on?

Do we need to obtain further specialist assessment?

Can we make a provisional diagnosis?

Compared with previous checklists has the pattern changed? If so, how and why?

Do we need to distribute the checklist information to other colleagues?

Do the supporting notes raise any questions or comments?

Do we broadly agree? If not, how do we interpret our differing perspectives?

Have we discussed the checklist with the parents? If not, when will this be done?

Have we discussed the checklist with the student? If not, when will this be done?

Discussion with colleagues – general discussion points

What other relevant information do we have about the student?

Do we need to find out more?

What extra insight can we add from our own experience of this student?

How has the student responded to previous intervention? What does this tell us?

Do we understand this type of special need? Do we need more information?

What are the key sources for information or expertise? How can we access them?

What is the evidence-based, 'best practice' for this student's special needs?

What are the parents' perspectives? What are their priorities?

What is the student's perspective? What are their own priorities?

Is there anything we have not covered?

Planning for the future

What are our goals for the next 3 months/6 months/12 months

What evidence-based best practice will be used in working towards the goals?

What benchmarks will we use to measure progress towards these goals?

What are the possible pitfalls in our plans? How can these be avoided?

How will we build on the positives? How will we know that we are making headway?

How will we involve the parents and the student in our planning and implementation?

How will we record the outcome of this meeting? Who will get copies?

GUIDE: DISCUSSING A STUDENT'S SPECIAL NEEDS WITH PARENTS AND CAREGIVERS

Parents and caregivers have a key role to play in making decisions about the child with special needs. Not only do they have a legal and moral right to be involved, they are also likely to have a unique insight and deep understanding of the child or adolescent's strengths and on the challenges they face.

Some parents may be confident and assertive when meeting with teachers, others may be uncomfortable, anxious or defensive. This is particularly so if they are worried about their child and uncertain of what options they may have.

Obviously an open and constructive discussion will help to build trust and understanding between parents and teachers, with the best interests of the child or adolescent as the driving force.

Preparing for a meeting

- Purpose of the meeting. Parents can be consulted when the agenda is being put together, so that there is agreement about what topics the meeting will cover.

- Who will attend? The student will often accompany the parents to the meeting. In which case the Discussion Guide for talking with a student should also be referred to. Parents may wish to bring along a relative, friend or professional as a support. This should be welcomed. Parents also need to know who will be at the meeting, including their names, their positions and roles in relationship to the student.

- Who will lead the discussion? It is important that the person who leads the discussion is aware of and responsive to the parent's perspectives. The person leading the meeting also needs to make sure that the parents have a fair chance to speak and that they are listened to respectfully.

- What questions should be raised? Suggested questions can be considered. Parents can be asked to bring prepared questions of their own to the meeting.

- What preparation needs to be done ahead of the meeting? Parents often have reports from other professionals which will help teachers.

- The checklists can be used in various ways:

  - Teachers can complete a checklist to be discussed with the parents at the meeting

  - Teacher and parents can work through a checklist together ahead of the meeting

  - Parents can complete a checklist by themselves ahead of the meeting

- How will the proceedings of the meeting be recorded? For small meetings a file note written by the convener may suffice. For more complex meetings appoint a competent minute taker. In all situations, if the parents attend the meeting they should be given a written record of the proceedings.

Discussion with parents – using the checklists

Looking at the checklist, what are the things that worry you most?

Looking at the checklist, what do you see as the positives?

Looking at what the teachers have put on the checklist, is there anything you see differently?

Is there anything not covered by the checklist that is important (good or bad)?

We are thinking that we need some more expert advice on this area; what do you think?

We are looking at what to do about this. We are considering . . . what do you think?

We see this as a strength; do you agree? How can we build on this?

Would you be interested in some supporting information? I'll get you a copy.

Would other people in your family agree with what you/the teachers have put down?

Discussion with parents – general discussion points

Do you have any medical or school reports from earlier years that might help us?

If you had to describe your child in just a few words, what would you say?

How do you think your child sees things? How does school seem from their perspective?

What do you think your child finds most difficult? At home? At school?

What do you see as your child's strengths? What are you proud of?

What does your child worry or get upset about?

What does your child enjoy most? At home? At school?

In school, what do you think has worked well in the past?

What has not worked in the past? Do you know why it was not a success?

Is there anyone outside of school who helps your child?

What are your biggest challenges in meeting your child's needs?

How do you deal with those challenges?

What would you like us to focus on in our support program for your child?

From what we have told you, what do you think about the plans we are making?

Is there anything further we can do to help you?

GUIDE: DISCUSSING THEIR SPECIAL NEEDS WITH A STUDENT

Wherever possible it is important to directly involve the student in discussions about their own special needs. Understanding the student's subjective experiences, opinions and feelings is fundamental to the process of meeting their special needs. Equally it is important for the student [as far as practicable] to understand the rationale for what is being planned.

Preparing for a meeting

- Purpose of the meeting. The student can be consulted when the discussion is being planned, so that they understand why they are meeting with the teacher/ counsellor and have a chance to say what they would like to discuss.

- Who will attend? A student may wish to bring along a parent, friend or professional as a support. This should be welcomed. Students also need to know who will be at the meeting, including their names and roles in the student's schooling. Sometimes a student will not be fully able to speak for themselves, in which case a parent or other adult can be invited as advocate and spokesperson.

- Who will lead the discussion? It is important that the person who leads the discussion has good rapport with the student and understands them well. The person leading the meeting also needs to make sure that the student (or their advocate) has a fair chance to speak and that they are listened to respectfully.

- What questions should be raised? Suggested questions can be considered. Students (or their advocates) can be asked to bring prepared questions of their own to the meeting.

- What preparation needs to be done ahead of the meeting? Teachers can collect relevant information ahead of the meeting.

- The checklists can be used in various ways:
  - Teacher/counsellor and student can go through a checklist together ahead of the meeting, each contributing their own insights
  - Teacher/counsellor and student can review the results of a checklist completed by other teachers ahead of the meeting
  - Teacher/counsellor can present a verbal summary of the key points from a school-based checklist ahead of the meeting
  - Parent and child/adolescent can go through a checklist together ahead of the meeting

- How will the proceedings of the meeting be recorded? For small meetings a file note written by the convener may suffice. For more complex meetings appoint a competent minute taker. A student and their parents can be given a summary of the meeting notes, or the full record as appropriate.

Discussion with a student – using the checklists

Looking at the checklist, what are the things that worry you most?
Looking at the checklist, what do you see as the positives?

Looking at what the teachers have put on the checklist, is there anything you see differently?

Looking at what your parents have put down on the checklist, is there anything you see differently?

Is there anything not covered by the checklist that is important (good or bad)?

We are looking at what to do about this. We are considering . . . what do you think?

We see this as a strength, do you agree? How can we build on this?

Discussion with a student – general discussion points

Is there anything that particularly worries you?

What do you find most difficult? At home? At school?

What are your strengths? What are you proud of?

What do worry or get upset about? At home? At school?

What do you enjoy most? At home? At school?

In school, what have teachers done that has helped you?

What has not worked?

What are your biggest challenges in school?

Which adults at school do you get along with best?

Which students at school do you get along with best?

How do you handle the things that are hard?

If you had three wishes what would they be?

What would you like us to focus on in our support program?

What do you think about the plans we are making?

Is there anything you really don't want us to try?

How can the school help you best?

FINDING THE RIGHT CHECKLIST

The following charts will help you decide which checklists to use. These charts can only offer an approximation of the potential classification as there are so many possibilities. The four charts cover the following categories:

Motivation and concentration difficulties
Social and behavioural difficulties
Learning difficulties
Communication difficulties

Choose the chart that you think is the best match for the student's pattern of difficulties. Photocopying single copies of the charts is permitted.

You will see there is a list of *Observed Behaviours* in the right-hand column of the chart. There is a series of diagnostic categories across the top of the chart.

1 Look at the first item in the *Observed Behaviours* list. Run your eye across the row and circle any cells that are shaded. Ignore any unshaded cells.

2 Move down to the next item in the list of *Observed Behaviours* and again circle any shaded cells that are in that row. Ignore any unshaded cells.

3 Repeat for the rest of the chart

4 If an *Observed Behaviour* does not apply then skip that row entirely and move onto the next.

5 If necessary, repeat the exercise on one of the other charts.

When you have completed the chart, you will be able to see if the cells you have circled fall into any particular column or diagnostic category. This then gives you a starting point for which checklist(s) to use.

Remember that a student may have more than one type of special need. Several disorders are known to occur together.

Other disorders may occur together just by chance, for instance, a gifted student might also be anxious or depressed. You may need to use two or more checklists if you suspect that the student has a complex pattern of difficulties.

Table 8.1

Finding the right checklist: motivation and concentration difficulties

Key to shading

	Possible
	Consider
	Definitely consider

Diagnostic Categories

Columns (left to right): Autism · Asperger Syndrome · Anxiety Disorder · Selective Mutism · Depression · Child abuse · ADHD (inattentive) · ADHD (hyperactive) · Conduct Disorder · Oppositional Defiant Disorder · Dyslexia · Dyscalculia · Intellectual Disability · Giftedness · Immaturity · Low self-esteem · Developmental Coordination Disorder

Observed Behaviours

- Does not settle to set tasks
- Slow to complete most class work
- Reluctant to persevere
- Complains of being bored
- Lacks confidence in own ability
- Seems to be in a world of their own
- Work is messy, looks careless
- Student does seem to aim for success
- Students says the work is too hard
- Impulsive, does not stop and think
- Student does not respond to rewards

Table 8.2

Finding the right checklist: social and behavioural difficulties

Key to shading	
	Possible
	Consider
	Definitely consider

Observed Behaviours / Diagnostic Categories	Autism	Asperger Syndrome	Anxiety Disorder	Selective Mutism	Depression	Maltreatment, abuse and bullying	ADHD (inattentive)	ADHD (hyperactive)	Conduct Disorder	Oppositional Defiant Disorder	Tourette Syndrome	Intellectual Disability	Giftedness	Immaturity	Low self-esteem
Has few if any friends	■	■								■		▨	▨		
Easily annoyed, loses temper					▨			▨	■	■					▨
Poor empathy with others	▨	■							■	▨			▨		
Does not obey instructions		▨						▨	■	■		▨		▨	
Easily upset by small setbacks		▨			▨					▨					▨
Overly dependent on adults or peers		▨	▨			▨	▨					▨		▨	
Withdrawn, reluctant to join in			▨						▨						
Bullies or harasses other students						▨			▨	▨					
Inflexible, can't 'go with the flow'	■	■	▨	▨						▨			▨		
Obsessed by unusual topics or objects	■	■								▨			▨		
Sexually inappropriate behaviour						■						▨			
Poor self-control								▨	■			▨			▨
Easily upset by trivial matters		▨		▨						▨				▨	▨
Calls out, makes inappropriate noises	▨							▨			■	▨	▨		

Table 8.3

Finding the right checklist: learning difficulties

Key to shading

(white)	Possible
(light grey)	Consider
(dark grey)	Definitely consider

Observed Behaviours \ Diagnostic Categories	Depression	ADHD (inattentive)	ADHD (hyperactive)	Dyslexia	Dyscalculia	Intellectual Disability	Speech and Language Disorders	Giftedness	Developmental Coordination Disorder
Finds it hard to understand topics						Definitely consider	Consider		
Working below age level across the curriculum	Consider	Consider	Consider	Consider	Consider	Consider	Consider		
Seems bright, underachieves in some areas	Consider			Definitely consider	Definitely consider		Consider	Consider	
Is not up to age standard with literacy				Definitely consider		Definitely consider	Consider		
Reading comprehension exceeds accuracy				Definitely consider		Definitely consider			
Reading accuracy exceeds comprehension						Definitely consider			
Inaccurate spelling				Definitely consider		Definitely consider			
Poor handwriting and book work				Definitely consider		Definitely consider			Definitely consider
Cannot put ideas down on paper				Definitely consider	Definitely consider	Definitely consider			Consider
Finds math concepts hard to understand					Definitely consider	Definitely consider	Consider		
Finds it hard to learn math facts and methods			Consider	Consider	Definitely consider	Definitely consider			
Results do not reflect effort put in	Consider			Definitely consider	Definitely consider	Definitely consider	Consider		

Table 8.4

Finding the right checklist: communication difficulties

Key to shading:

Shading	Meaning
(white)	
(light grey)	Possible
(medium grey)	Consider
(dark)	Definitely consider

Observed Behaviours / Diagnostic Categories	Asperger Syndrome	Anxiety Disorder	Selective Mutism	ADHD (inattentive)	ADHD (hyperactive)	Tourette Syndrome	Intellectual Disability	Speech and Language Disorders	Giftedness	Developmental Coordination Disorder
Misunderstands instructions or requests							Definitely	Definitely		
Does not understand metaphors or jokes	Definitely						Definitely			
Not good at reading nonverbal language	Definitely						Consider			
Needs information to be repeated				Consider	Consider		Definitely	Definitely		
Inattentive when others are speaking				Definitely	Definitely		Definitely	Definitely		
Poor conversational skills with others	Definitely						Consider	Consider		
Reluctant to speak when asked to do so		Consider	Definitely				Definitely	Definitely		
Does not explain things well	Definitely						Definitely	Definitely		
Speaks 'like a professor'									Definitely	
Speech is unclear or difficult to understand										Definitely
Mispronounces some words										Definitely
Has trouble 'getting words out', stutters										Definitely
Makes inappropriate noises						Definitely				
Swears or repeats words over & over						Definitely				
Has trouble finding the right word								Possible		
Has a 'foreign' accent (although not foreign)	Definitely									

Index

Printed in Great Britain
by Amazon

17085410R00115